Southern Literary Studies
Louis D. Rubin, Jr., Editor

The Achievement *of* Cormac McCarthy

The Achievement of Cormac McCarthy

VEREEN M. BELL

Louisiana State University Press
Baton Rouge

Published by Louisiana State University Press
lsupress.org

Copyright © 1988 by Louisiana State University Press
All rights reserved. Except in the case of brief quotations used in
articles or reviews, no part of this publication may be reproduced
or transmitted in any format or by any means without written
permission of Louisiana State University Press.

Louisiana Paperback Edition, 2023

Designer: Laura Roubique Gleason
Typeface: Trump Mediaeval
Typesetter: Composing Room of Michigan, Inc.

Library of Congress Cataloging-in-Publication Data

Bell, Vereen M., 1934–
    The achievement of Cormac McCarthy / Vereen M. Bell.
    p. cm.
    Bibliography: p.
    Includes index.
    ISBN 978-0-8071-1408-7 (cloth : alk. paper) | ISBN 978-0-8071-8037-2
    (paperback) | ISBN 978-0-8071-8131-7 (epub) | ISBN 978-0-8071-8135-5 (pdf)
    I. McCarthy, Cormac, 1933–   —Criticism and Interpretation.
I. Title.
PS3563.C337Z58 1988
813'.54—dc19   88-5906
                                                      CIP

Grateful acknowledgment is made to Random House, Inc., for permission
to quote from the following works by Cormac McCarthy: *The Orchard Keeper*,
copyright © 1965 by Cormac McCarthy; *Outer Dark*, copyright © 1968 by Cormac
McCarthy; *Child of God*, copyright © 1973 by Cormac McCarthy; *Blood Meridian*, copyright © 1985 by Cormac McCarthy; and *Suttree*, copyright © 1979 by
Cormac McCarthy.

For Mother and Bill

Contents

Preface xi
Introduction: The Mystery of Being 1
I Beyond the Pale: *The Orchard Keeper* 10
II Word and Flesh: *Outer Dark* 33
III The Ambiguities of Innocence: *Child of God* 53
IV Death and Affirmation: *Suttree* 69
V The Metaphysics of Violence: *Blood Meridian* 116
Bibliography 137
Index 141

Preface

Cormac McCarthy is as elusive in life as life is in his fictions. He is a relatively young man, born in 1933, and little is known of him. His novels are scarcely read, even in Tennessee, his more-or-less native state. But both labor and obscurity seem to agree with him. He is a meticulous, unhurried craftsman and yet declines flatly to promote his own work, and he indirectly gives offense by disdaining academic patronage. His contemporary, Thomas Pynchon, has managed to protect his privacy while achieving both fame and fortune; the fact that McCarthy has had to be content with only privacy says less about the quality or the nature of his work than it does about the irony of postmodernism's absorption into the mainstream of American intellectual life. McCarthy's five novels, *The Orchard Keeper* (1965), *Outer Dark* (1968), *Child of God* (1973), *Suttree* (1979), and *Blood Meridian* (1985), have sold probably no more than fifteen thousand copies altogether in their original Random House editions. Paperback editions of *The Orchard Keeper* (1982), *Outer Dark* (1984), *Child of God* (1984), and *Blood Meridian* (1986) are now available, thanks to the intelligent reclamation efforts of Daniel Halpern and the Ecco Press. *Suttree* is now available in a Vintage Contemporaries paperback from Random House (1986). (Except for *Suttree*, for which I have used the Vintage Contemporaries edition, the texts cited hereinafter are the Ecco Press editions.) McCarthy, meanwhile, having no other profession and earning virtually no income from his novels, remains committed to writing well and therefore patiently, aided intermittently by foundation support, including a substantial grant from the MacArthur Foundation. His mission as a novelist has been endorsed by such disparate gentry as Saul Bellow, Robert Coles, Ralph Ellison, Robert Penn Warren, Anatole Broyard, and Guy Davenport. He is a writer whom other writers respect and envy especially, because he transforms the language with power. He has the rare gift of a style that is photorealistic in its precision and yet charismatically rich and suggestive. His language brings the real world back to us replenished but still familiar, as if we were seeing it truly for the first time. He is a novelist of profound, even dark, moral seriousness who seems to be motivated most deeply by a humane, comic stoicism. He is a major writer in all of the conventional senses of the word, our best unknown major writer by many measures.

He has often been said to be influenced by William Faulkner and Flannery O'Connor. That influence is obvious because McCarthy without embarrassment lets it be, in fact forces it toward our attention both as an homage and as a means of positioning himself in a hypothetical American pantheon. The declared kinship says, first, I am not Donald Barthelme or Norman Mailer but, then, I am not Faulkner or O'Connor either; though I live in the same place, I am no more like either of them than they are like each other; and I am not behind but beside them. The novels themselves vividly confirm McCarthy's confidence in his independent position and purpose, and it is therefore their uniqueness that we respond to most intimately. In fact, part of the problem McCarthy has with his readership may be this very uncategorizable quality, which makes certain Aristotelian temperaments uneasy, as it did with Faulkner when Faulkner himself was unread.

Even if the world wished to beat a path to McCarthy's door, it would be hard-pressed to find it. McCarthy spent his childhood and early manhood in Knoxville and its surrounding rural Appalachian mountain areas. His family moved to Tennessee from Rhode Island when he was a young child, his father as a lawyer for the Tennessee Valley Authority. Cormac—originally Charles but renamed by his family for the Irish king—was raised a Roman Catholic in decidedly Protestant territory. He returns now and then to the Knoxville area, where his wife and children live and where he has lifelong friends. Otherwise he seems not to live anywhere in particular; nor does he seem to want to. Chicago, Las Vegas, New Orleans, London, Paris, and various border towns in Texas and Mexico are some of the places that have held him longest. El Paso has been his most recent home. Although he is a disciplined writer, he keeps moving, responding to the novelty of new settings. He is said to work mainly in motels and to live austerely. He attended the University of Tennessee in Knoxville but dropped out twice and never finished a degree program. He has dropped out of a lot of things with the persistence of a man who clearheadedly knows, eventually at least, what he wants to do and what he doesn't.

In the process of remaining only a writer and having, so to speak, transcended domestication in its many forms, he has preserved an unusually direct and unmediated access to other people's experience. That experience enters his language with a freshness and vividness that draws our attention as much as the subject itself. McCarthy's prose can be so exact that it seems artificial, and his style ranges amazingly from plainest human speech to a dense, polyphonic rhetoric. (In this respect he is Faulkner's true heir, and Joyce's and Eliot's as well.) His ear for the nuances of human speech is so perfectly pitched that he writes dialogue nonchalantly without the net of inverted commas. He is obedient to the claims of the physical world. The texture of the world in his novels is dense and specific; the moral and intellectual implications of experience are left intriguingly vague, always eluding the reification of thought.

Writing about McCarthy is an oddly embarrassing project because one is always saying either more or less than needs to be said, and always, in any case, in a version of the language that by comparison with McCarthy's seems poignantly inept. But McCarthy needs to be written about, both because his work is major work and yet still unknown and because he himself is so unwilling—in his work and outside it—to meet his readers halfway. The object of the chapters that follow, then, is to close up some of the space between the uncompromising novelist and his uncourted audience. This study of McCarthy's work has no thesis other than that which issues from the cryptic intelligibility of the novels themselves when they are patiently and attentively considered. One strength of McCarthy's novels is that they resist the imposition of theses from the outside, especially conventional ones, and that they seem finally to call all theses into question. With such a novelist critical discourse is hard to get started, but once it is started it seems destined to go on.

The Achievement *of* Cormac McCarthy

Introduction: The Mystery of Being

On the last page of *Outer Dark*, one of the roads, among many, that Culla Holme is aimlessly traveling comes abruptly to a portentous dead end.

> Late in the day the road brought him into a swamp. And that was all. Before him stretched a spectral waste out of which reared only the naked trees in attitudes of agony and dimly hominoid like figures in a landscape of the damned. A faintly smoking garden of the dead that tended away to the earth's curve. He tried his foot in the mire before him and it rose in a vulvate welt claggy and sucking. He stepped back. A stale wind blew from this desolation and the marsh reeds and black ferns among which he stood clashed softly like things chained. He wondered why a road should come to such a place. (p. 242)

The prevailing gothic and nihilistic mood of all of Cormac McCarthy's novels is condensed in this passage, and for this particular novel it contributes an appropriately unaccommodating resolution to an otherwise inconclusive and highly unconventional narrative. The passage and the whole event function also as a grim, self-referential joke. The novel, a story of two separate but associated journeys made by Culla Holme and his sister, Rinthy, has led us nowhere. All of its thematic implications have been left suspended, its mysteries—narrative and metaphysical—deepened but never clarified. Each promise of direction and understanding has been thwarted. Metaphorically a road is the equivalent of a signifier in language or structure: it points us in a direction and leads us somewhere that could reasonably be anticipated to be a vicinity of meaning. But the roads of McCarthy's novels, *Outer Dark* in particular, do not do that. The point in the novels of the alternating lurid and lyrical events seems to be precisely that roads are helpful to us only as long as we believe they are taking us somewhere but that in the long run they don't: that real moral experience does not lend itself to reassuring thematic paraphrase.

All of McCarthy's novels are characterized by this perverse and tantalizing density. The pressure of meaning in them is strong, but they belligerently resist abstraction and classification. They appear, in fact, to resist abstraction on purpose and to move instead toward some more primal epistemology, toward a knowledge of origins before a bicameral brain enabled us—or compelled us—to begin to sort things out. Conceptual experience, in other words, is "bracketed"; eidetic experience flourishes and flashes vivid signals because it is not subsumed into doctrine or ideology. Not meaning itself but the traditional idea of meaning is made obsolete. The earth is, as Wallace Stevens said, "cleared of its stiff and stubborn, man-locked set."

This antimetaphysical bias is inescapable in McCarthy's novels because of the concreteness of his prose style: it binds us to the phenomenal world. It is as lapidary and particular as John Updike's, though less ideational and less self-conscious by a factor of, say, ten, and therefore, in its strange economy of effect, more suggestive. Even labored and latinate passages such as the description of the swamp are, when analyzed, cleanly referential and descriptive—as opposed to many of Faulkner's, for example, which they deceptively resemble. Such passages, which recur with calculated frequency, are dense and portentous mainly because of the high ratio of metaphor in them, not because they introduce new levels of abstraction. Risking extravagance, they serve to keep us from subsiding into a merely naturalistic perceptual realm. They keep a dreamlike, almost symbolist, pressure of meaning, or meaningfulness, alive in the text without providing easy or even perceptible means of release. They are necessary, in other words, to give McCarthy's otherwise concrete world its aura of mysterious, opaque, and unyielding signification.

Simpler events presented in a simpler style also generate the same complex environment of suggestion. One such is this remarkable, prolonged episode describing Rinthy Holmes as she washes up and prepares for bed in the plain house of a family of country people who have taken her in for the night.

> When they had done in the kitchen she followed the woman down the passageway at the rear of the house, the woman holding the lamp before them and so out into the cool night air and across the boardfloored dogtrot, the door falling to behind them and the woman opening the next one and entering, her close behind, a whippoorwill calling from nearby for just as long as they passed through the open and hushing instantly with the door's closing. (pp. 61–62)

She opened the door and the night air came upon them again sweetly through the warm reek of the room, the whippoorwill calling more distant, the door closing and the woman's steps fading across the dogtrot and the bird once again more faintly, or perhaps another bird, beyond the warped and waney boards and thin yellow flame that kept her from the night. (p. 62)

The whippoorwill had stopped and she bore with her now in frenzied colliding orbits about the lamp chimney a horde of moths and night insects. (p. 63)

She put the lamp on the shelf and sat on the bed. It was a shuck tick and collapsed slowly beneath her with a dry brittle sound and a breath of stale dust. She turned down the lamp and removed her dress and hung it over the brass bedpost. Then she unrolled the shift and put it on and crawled into the bed.... When they were all turned in they lay in the hot silence and listened to one another breathing. She turned carefully on her rattling pallet. She listened for a bird or for a cricket. Something she might know in all that dark. (pp. 64–65)

This sequence of scenes takes up five pages in the text and involves nothing more than Rinthy's washing and going to bed, interrupted only by an uneventful encounter with the family's son outside. The episode is autonomous and involves no foreshadowing. Rinthy is not in danger in this place—quite the reverse—but the description of her progress is charged with the sense of the vivid strangeness of strange places and, by extension, with the strangeness of being itself once it ceases to be familiar. Rhythm, recurrence, and McCarthy's assured selection of detail do most of this work. A wholly ordinary event has in effect been transformed into a metaphor for the mystery of experience, and yet the tenor and vehicle of it are not separable. This experience is not only alive and immediate, it is invigorated with possibility as well. The style is concrete and grounded but resists closure.

In McCarthy's novels, in other words, the world itself is mysterious enough without involving ideas or transcendence of it. The world is convincingly present to us, material but more than usually real. We experience it at eye level with or through the characters, and this eye-level progress enhances empathy on the one hand and militates against abstraction and formulation on the other. If the Knoxville of the early 1950s were still there, had not been razed, that is, to make way for a brave new commercial world and a new expressway, one could walk its back streets on the west side today with a copy of *Suttree* in hand as confidently as one walks James Joyce's Dublin or the London of Moll Flanders. McCarthy's earlier novels, which are set in rural Tennessee, south of Knoxville, are cartographically much vaguer, but that is a main difference to begin with between the city and the country, where the contours of both space and time are more generous.

But the power of physical detail is the same in all of the novels; and whether or not we know precisely where we are in a given text, we have a vivid sensation of what it is like being there under those circumstances and of nothing—no essence or inference or idea—being truer or mattering more. McCarthy's first four novels are set within a hundred-mile radius of Maryville, Tennessee, and convey to us vividly the speech, manners, and values of the area's people, the climate, the nature of the land, its animals living their own separate life—the specific whole ecology and spirit of a region. When the scene shifts in *Blood Meridian* to Mexico and the American Southwest, it is as if this exotic desert region had been his home for the whole of his natural life. We are reminded again that experience is primarily not universal but particular, that we live not in an outline but in a place.

Ordinarily the omniscient narrator in McCarthy's novels is recessive—merely narrating—and the characters are almost without thoughts, certainly without thought processes, so neither narrator nor characters offer us any help with the business of generalizing. Except in *Blood Meridian*, no normative characters are available to speak the point—no disguised English teachers like those in Saul Bellow's novels or Walker Percy's; and even in *Blood Meridian*, the exceptional case, the thematic discourse is like a dark parody of such idioms, the antithesis of what the evidence of the surrounding text represents. McCarthy's novels are otherwise about as un-Jamesian as it is possible for fiction to be in this post-Jamesian dispensation. The motivation of characters is usually tantalizingly obscure. Culla Holme, for instance, says—three times—that he is looking for his sister, but he is not doing that very effectively; he never asks after her as he moves from one town to the next, so we can never be really sure what he is doing or what keeps him moving. All of the characters threaten to become almost eerily unselfconscious. This is a poignant and haunting effect in itself, calling forth an impoverishment in them far deeper than their simple lack of material means. Oddly, this vacuum also invites empathy on our part, since, again, we are seeing mainly through their eyes rather than observing and assaying their thoughts. But it also ensures that—allowing for the extra data available to us—we remain as mystified and as suspended as they are in a seemingly perpetual hermeneutic adventure.

One reason that meaning does not prevail over narrative and texture is that the characters whose experience we share are for the most part solitary and unsocialized; they are therefore wholly indifferent to discourse and have no interest in ideas about how societies are sustained and kept coherent. Most of them, though sociable enough when called upon, seem in some uncommon, fundamental way to want to be left alone; they find solitude and isolation the normal conditions. In the first three novels they are also rural people who exhibit a characteristic rural fatalism about issues of cause and effect: existence is no more explicable to them than climate, or nature itself, and not a fruitful subject of meditation. They do not thrust into the future; in fact, future hardly exists for them, and this odd circumstance does odd things to the narrative flow. Events, characters, phrases rhyme with each other in such a way that we seem to move forward and backward in time simultaneously. The past remains alive in the present in the many related stories of the region, of place, stories within stories, which produce a dreamlike redundancy of effect and an eerie illusion of depth and spatiality inherent in the nature of time.

Typically, in fact, the passage of time is not charted for us at all. The relationship of events is not organized according to a conventional time scheme; blank spaces prevail where we might expect "shortly thereafter" or "several months later" to be. There is rarely any sure way of knowing whether a day has passed or a year. We are, so to speak, locked-through the experience of the characters, as if through a canal. The characters in turn dwell firmly and intensely on whatever spot they happen to be on, surviving, economizing with what they are given, trusting—in spite of gruesome indications to the contrary—some mysterious principle of buoyancy in the world to keep them up. Reproducing the quality of this experience in this setting and at this level seems to be McCarthy's highest compositional priority, and it is therefore the episodic nature of experience itself that is in the foreground rather than what it leads to or how our moral natures are shaped by it or what principles might be inferred from it. Hence, too, the pace of the novels is agrarian—methodically slow—and frequently even that pace is slowed down, on both a cinematic and Faulknerian model, so that much detail and space crowd into small units of time.

When we are presented with experience in this oddly formal way, what we are forced to look at is as often brutal and loathsome as it is exhilarating and gratifying; but we are not permitted to avert our gaze, as we would in real life. McCarthy's prose both distances us and draws us into a renewed world where the primordial has remained both rich and strange.

> Late that afternoon the high sheriff of Sevier County with two deputies and two other men crossed the field from Willy Gibson's old rifle shop where they'd left the car and crossed the creek and went up the old log road. They carried lanterns and coils of rope and a number of muslin shrouds on which was stenciled Property of the State of Tennessee. The high sheriff of Sevier County himself descended into the sink and surveyed the mausoleum there. The bodies were covered with adipocere, a pale gray cheesy mold common to corpses in damp places, and scallops of light fungus grew along them as they do on logs rotting in the forest. The chamber was filled with sour smell, a faint reek of ammonia. The sheriff and the deputy made a noose from a rope and they slipped it around the upper body of the first corpse and drew it tight. They pulled her from the slab and dragged her across the stone floor of the vault and down a corridor to where daylight fell against the wall of the sink. In this leaning bole of light, standing there among the shifting motes, they called for a rope. When it descended they made it fast to the rope about the corpse and called aloft again. The rope drew taut and the first of the dead sat up on the cave floor, the hands that hauled the rope above sorting the shadows like puppeteers. Gray soapy clots of matter fell from the cadaver's chin. She ascended dangling. She sloughed in the weem of the noose. A gray rheum dripped.
> In the evening a jeep descended the log road towing a trailer in the bed of which lay seven bodies bound in muslin like enormous hams. As they went down the valley in the new fell dark basking nighthawks rose from the dust in the road before them with wild wings and eyes red as jewels in the headlights. (*Child of God*, pp. 196–197)

A characteristically careful arrangement of details gives this passage its unsettling suggestion of a theme: Willy Gibson's old rifle shop, the bureaucratically functional body bags, the pedantic, textbook definition of *adipocere*, the bound bodies resembling grocery-store hams, the complete absence of any sense of human personality. The passage compels us to wonder how, when we see everything at once, anything can be understood alone, and yet nothing so banal as that even breaks the surface as discourse; and at the end the beauty of the hawks and even the roll of the sentence that conveys them to us seems to allude to some irreducible beauty always just beyond thought at the heart of the world. Essentially the corpses, the jeeps, and the basking hawks are all. When the world is perceived innocent of moral form in this way, it stands forth in language vividly and, for better or worse, thrives there. It would be difficult to imagine Cormac McCarthy in discourse with Walter Pater, but it is not altogether inane to conceive that he has subscribed to Pater's unideological ideology and adapted it to what might have been thought to be a wholly new and inhospitable environment.

> It might even be said that our failure is to form habits: for, after all, habit is relative to a stereotyped world, and meantime it is only the roughness of the eye that makes any two persons, things, situations, seem alike. While all melts under our feet, we may well grasp at any exquisite passion, or any contribution to knowledge that seems by a lifted horizon to set the spirit free for a moment, or any stirring of the senses . . . or work of the artist's hands, or the face of one's friend. Not to discriminate every moment some passionate attitude in those about us, and in the very brilliancy of their gifts some tragic dividing of forces on their ways, is, on this short day of frost and sun, to sleep before evening. With this sense of the splendor of our experience and of its awful brevity, gathering all we are into one desperate effort to see and touch, we shall hardly have time to make theories about the things we see and touch. (Walter Pater, "Conclusion," *Studies in the History of the Renaissance*)

McCarthy sharpens the focus upon the pockets of experience by employing a modernist, elliptical narrative technique. (In his fusion of traditional materials with modernist narrative method he is closely allied with Faulkner.) Reading a McCarthy novel for the first time and bringing conventional expectations of narrative to it will cause one to be misled—deliberately probably—and even mystified. Book-spanning plots are promised but turn out not to exist. Subjects exist, *données*, and chronological advance is always perceptible; but plots in the conventional sense, complicated stories with appropriate resolutions or outcomes, do not prevail. Even when a summarizable plot does take hold, as in *Child of God*, its outline is subordinated to smaller units of anecdote, to stories within stories that carry attention to the edges of the main stream. McCarthy's tendency to work in these small anecdotal units that tend not to connect up with each other would seem at first to militate against visibility of theme. But in the long run it expresses what theme there is, and in the appropriate structural form.

Life's way in the world of these novels is dialectical, contingent, and transient. In the background of the novels there may be a residual yearning for ontological certainty —we suspect this from the recurrence of preachers and priests, however demented. But this nostalgia is subordinated forcefully to the opposing conviction, implied everywhere, that absolute certainty is always a form of unfreedom; that an administered world is, for the individual, a deprived one; that ideas and systems, the pursuit of essences and of first principles, are as dangerous and as reifying as imposed social orders. So the structures are emblematic as well as functional: it is in the pockets of experience, in the particular, that we in fact live. Human life is therefore most accurately revealed to us through anecdote and incident rather than through types.

Rinthy Holme in *Outer Dark* is representative of characters who, as McCarthy puts it in one place, know things raw, "unshaped by the constructions of a mind obsessed with form" (*Suttree*, p. 427). We do not know where she and her brother live when the novel opens; we know virtually nothing about their parents, and neither does she. The two of them inhabit an austere, rural void. When Culla, leaving for a brief period, warns her not to take in strangers, she replies, "They ain't a soul in this world but what is a stranger to me" (p. 29). When she sets out in search of her newborn child, which Culla, its father, has left to die in the woods, she doesn't know whether she is headed toward town or away from it because she's never been there. When she is asked by a suspicious farmer whether she hasn't run off from somewhere she says, "No . . . I ain't even got nowheres to run off from" (p. 101). She says to a doctor later, "I don't live nowhere no more. . . . I never did much. I just go around huntin my chap" (p. 156). Hunting her "chap" entails hunting a deranged tinker who has found and taken her abandoned baby; but she has never seen the tinker and he has never seen her, and she does not even know, until a storekeeper tells her, that there are "all different kinds" (p. 75). She has no reason to choose one road over another since the tinker could be anywhere.

Her quest proceeds in a vacuum that is intermittently filled by sympathetic country people who help her out but seem, though they have homes and families, no less wandering in space than she. She is shrewd and strong and humorous, but she is virtually without thoughts, driven on and sustained by the simple meaning that she makes. Both grounded and unearthly, she is an austere paradigm of human life in McCarthy's paradigmless world.

In *The Orchard Keeper* Arthur Ownby is described by a welfare agent in a kind of bureaucratic oxymoron as an "anomic type." He has been misrelegated to a state mental hospital after a feisty encounter with the law. But he is a hero in his novel, one of three, *because* he is anomic; and his ludicrous fate at the hands of well-meaning representatives of the social order is symbolic—and for him worse than death. Cornelius Suttree, in his novel, learns, during a grisly, delirious battle with typhoid fever, that "God is not a thing. Nothing ever stops moving" (p. 461). He tells this to a priest who has come to tend him. He reports to the same priest that he has learned that there is one "Suttree and one Suttree only" (p. 461), meaning, among other things, that life is short and that there is no transcendent ego. He has dreamed of being voided into "a cold dimension without time without space and where all was motion" (p. 452). This gives us McCarthy's metaphysic summarized: none, in effect—no first principles, no foundational truth, Heraclitus without Logos. In each of these novels existence not only precedes but precludes essence. But if essence has been precluded, the human dream of it has not, so the pressure of meaningfulness remains even where meaning will not separate out. This may be why the characters themselves seem so human and other-than-human at the same time, both vividly of their small worlds and strangely otherworldly also, as if life beyond thought were itself only and yet our elusive dream of it as well.

I

Beyond the Pale
The Orchard Keeper

The Orchard Keeper, as its title suggests, is an elegy commemorating a doomed way of life; it is also a lament for the impermanence of human life generally and a meditation upon the irrelevance of the human in the impersonal scheme of things. In both respects its tone and values are of distant Anglo-Saxon origin. A stretch of portentous writing at the end reminds us of this—of time's indifference to human striving and achievement—after all the story's fates have been settled.

> The dead sheathed in the earth's crust and turning the slow diurnal of the earth's wheel, at peace with eclipse, asteroid, the dusty novae, their bones brindled with mold and the celled marrow going to frail stone, turning, their fingers laced with roots, at one with Tut and Agamemnon, with the seed and the unborn. (pp. 244–45)

So stated, the point is simultaneously clinical and sentimental; but it seems worth the risk in order for McCarthy to grant his characters a legitimate dignity by association, since one of the points he wishes his modest narrative to make is that heroic authority is not determined wholly by historical or mythic text.

That conventional notion, in turn, takes its resonance from the other theme of the passage, which reminds us, for the last time in the novel, that our human status in the world is provisional and that our genuinely enduring continuity with it is ironically inhuman, elemental, and complete. Ordinary as this thought is, it is hardly thinkable; and yet McCarthy's language brushes close enough also, for example, to Wordsworth's Lucy poems to remind us that others have thought it. Wordsworth's Lucy was willingly a solitary child of nature and celebrated in her elliptical story for that reason, as McCarthy's characters are in theirs. The cold irony, therefore, of being reclaimed and recycled in both texts is the same: "rolled round in earth's diurnal course / with rocks, and stones, and trees." In *The Orchard Keeper* this irony prevails as both a mood and a theme. The orchard itself is an aspect of the process, once a productive negotiation between man and nature, now untended, slowly falling into ruin, going back.

This first novel of McCarthy's is like his others in that it uses the Appalachian setting he knows best to represent and celebrate life beyond the pale. The phrase *beyond the pale* is one he uses; and it is worth pausing over, for the idea inherent in it is metaphorically central to everything McCarthy has written. In fifteenth-century Ireland *beyond the pale* meant outside the jurisdiction of the English monarch—hence, to the English and in fact, unadministered and uncivilized. As the idea has relevance to McCarthy's fiction, it refers not simply to the stubbornly unsocialized east Tennessee mountain people about whom he writes but also to the environment they inhabit, which is altogether unhuman. In approaching McCarthy for the first time it is essential to grasp the importance of this dual focus, since without acknowledging its relation to what R. P. Blackmur would have called the theoretic form of McCarthy's novels, their technical form can seem wholly mystifying.

By Jamesian standards *The Orchard Keeper* is a shambles. There is no ruling point of view, since there are not, by modernist standards, any thinking characters. The shifts from one point of view to another and from one story line to another are unpredictable, guided by no apparent logic. The story lines themselves are only tenuously connected to one another, and even then mainly by common theme rather than by character relationship or plot. (Deepening replication is the first principle of McCarthy's universe.) It would seem at times that the novel is taunting us in this respect. The first few pages, for instance, are presented from the point of view of a character who is killed thirty pages later and remains more or less visibly dead throughout the novel. Even the assurance we have in our point of view as readers—in collusion with the implied author pointing the way—is frequently and ingeniously turned against us.

Late in section II of the novel, for example, the old recluse, Arthur Ownby, after prolonged consideration, determines to put his mark upon a mysterious government tank that has been installed in the remote wooded area near his house and the abandoned orchard. To him it is an encroachment upon his isolation by the world he rejects, and one evening he ritualistically fires twelve partially "circumcized" shotgun shells into the wall of the tank in the shape of a crude letter X. It seems clear, partly because we are reading a novel, that he will eventually be discovered by the authorities and apprehended. When we next see Ownby, a thick snow has come into the mountains and he is characteristically and peacefully absorbed in the silent spectacle. This interval then concludes at a section break with what appears to be an ominous image: "Scout [his dog] was standing in snow to his belly, gazing out at the fantastic landscape with his bleary eyes. Across the yard, brilliant against the facade of pines beyond, a cardinal shot like a drop of blood" (p. 133). After the break, the next sentence is this: "There were three of them coming up the trackless road past the house, and two dogs." Unmistakably the three men are the agents of the law whom we have expected. But, to our surprise, they turn out to be not agents of the law at all and not even men, but boys—young John Wesley Rattner's three friends—happily rabbit hunting with their bouncing beagles. And the house is not Ownby's at all but John Wesley's—and it is now, suddenly, John Wesley's point of view.

The effect is remarkable, because here and in the appealing episodes that follow we are displaced from our authority as readers of a novel and put into an unsupervised free world—or rather into a world that is supervised according to more subtle narrative principles. This mode of organization implies a moving and committed trust in the world that, in turn, is communicated to us and becomes infectious.

McCarthy is expert at manipulating the conventions of reading, setting us up frequently so as to require us to consider some of the main differences between books and the world. One other such instance is the small narrative segment in which John Wesley and his mother come to terms with the fact that his father is no doubt dead. They know only that he has disappeared. He has in fact been killed in a fight with a man (Marion Sylder, who later befriends John Wesley) whose car he has tried to steal. When it becomes clear that he is not going to return home, Mrs. Rattner determines in her mind that he is dead and begins to conceive for him a pathetically wrongheaded mythic identity.

> If he'd lived, she told him one evening, you wouldn't want for nothin. And him disabled in the war with that platmium plate in his head and all—turned down the govmint disability, he did. Too proud. Wouldn't take no handout from nobody even if it was the govmint. He was a provider all right, may the Lord God Jesus keep him.

Yes, she said, eying him doubtfully, you make half the man he was an you'll be goin some. (pp. 72–73)

Having achieved this fiction, she is then compelled by its logic to flesh out the story and enjoin John Wesley to avenge his father's death.

> You goin to hunt him out. When you're old enough. Goin to find the man that took away your daddy....
> How can I? He had begun to cry.
> Your daddy'd of knowed how. He was a God-fearin man if he never took much to church meetin.... The Lord'll show you, boy. He will not forsake them what believe. Pray and the way will be made known to ye. He... You *swear* it, boy. (pp. 66–67)

Here we recognize a plot stirring, and a familiar one at that. But stir is all it does. It ends here. The boy does not forget, but what he remembers is only his mother's garbled grief. He does not set out on an oathbound quest to seek and avenge. Instead he loses both interest and curiosity, as any healthy real boy would, and goes about his boy's business: listening to the ducks in the mist on the pond, admiring the glaze of the frost in the sunrise, watching flocks of geese migrate across the horizon. It is his mother who is trapped in a plot; he himself is unbookishly free.

Huge stretches of narrative are ruled by no point of view whatever—long, densely descriptive passages that seem to bring what there is of a narrative to a dead halt: descriptions of implacable mountain weather, of a flooding stream, of a scavenging, desperate cat making her demented progress from one source of food to another, all the while being stalked herself by a great owl. At such times the human narrative spreads out as if into a delta, then recovers its shape, only to disperse again farther on. It may be that McCarthy is doing the best he can to construct a well-made novel and is amateurishly failing, but that seems unlikely. The technical form coincides too exactly with the theoretic form that underlies it. The high level of seemingly unassimilated raw material represents for us the ascendancy of the world-in-itself, the natural world, outside the jurisdiction of human forms; and for the three main characters who are associated in different ways with that mysterious and indifferent presence—Marion Sylder, John Wesley Rattner, Arthur Ownby—it is an exhilarating, chosen habitat. Between these characters and the unmetaphorical setting is played out a strong and believing representation of how the human and the emphatically not-human productively intersect.

A Jamesian point of view—or even modernist, crosscutting versions of it, as in the novels, say, of Virginia Woolf—makes for a very human world. This one is different not only technically but ontologically, a world without a point of view and without the temporary reassurances of an aesthetic illusion of one. The absence of a point of view in this world is one of the sources of its mystery and power, and the characters in the book who are whole are the ones attuned to it, paying the price of solitude for their freedom. Ethically they are children in effect—boys at three different ages of man—impervious to community spirit and civil law. "Cats is smart," says Arthur Ownby, the novel's uneducated elder statesman, declaring both what he knows and what he is. "They'll tear up anything they come up on, a cat will. Housecats is smart too. Smarter'n a dog or a mule. Folks thinks they ain't on account of you cain't learn em nothin, but what it is is that they won't learn nothin. They too smart" (p. 227). The decentralized narrative and occasional correspondence between the animals and the human figures in the novel are signs that the book is to be not about the ultimate sanctity of community values but about their irrelevance and about that end of the spectrum of human nature closest to the undomesticated natural world. The book itself is thus a tribute to the fact that little of the world is human and known and to its strange resistance to closure.

Both structurally and stylistically the human story is set in an animal context rather than vice versa. Wild cats, to whom Arthur Ownby superstitiously attributes ghostly powers, call out in the hollows near his house at night, distressing his peace. One of them appears periodically to look in at him in the darkness through the window of his room. A "tall gaunt hound" comes to stare in at John Wesley in his bed, stands there without moving, then goes away (pp. 64–65). In both cases it is as if the two modest human settlements had intruded upon a curious but unintimidated animal world. The log house John Wesley and his mother live in he manages to make seem as much like an animal's den as a human dwelling, scurrying into and out of its gable window like a night creature after his mother is asleep. It is literally and symbolically remote from civil jurisdiction.

> They paid no tax on it, for it did not exist in the county courthouse records, nor on the land, for they did not own it. They paid no rent on either house

or land, as claimants to either or both properties were nonexistent in deed as the house itself. (p. 63)

And to the boy's continuing wonder and satisfaction their human status in this place is tenuous.

> In the summer wasps nested over the boards, using the auger-holes where dowels had shrunk in some old dry weather and fallen to the floor to emerge out into the hot loft and drone past his bed to the window where a corner of glass was gone and so out into the sunlight. There had been mud-dobber nests stacked up the wide planks too but his mother had raked them all down one day and aside from the wasps there were only the borers and woodworms, which he never saw but knew by the soft cones of wood-dust that gathered on the floor, the top log beneath the eaves, or trailed down upon the cobwebs, heavy yellow sheets of them opaque with dust and thick as muslin. (pp. 62–63)

The sense in this one image of a resourceful, prevailing, invisible life persists through the book in all its settings and remains thematically its first point of reference. John Wesley's practically wordless life seems guided exclusively by the need to become subsumed into that mysterious and wordless world. Some of his adventures with his friends Warn Pulliam, Boog, and Johnny Romines take place inside a network of caves, where they are fascinated by the primitive forms and gravely consider the alternatives to being white. They and "Uncle Ather"—telling stories and sharing muscadine wine—are referred to as troglodytes, which in some sense they are. One afternoon John Wesley catches a bass from the willows "in water not a foot deep" and cleans it and holds the tiny heart in the palm of his hand and watches it "still beating" (p. 66).

The lives of the four boys, independently of one another and together, seem to revolve exclusively around their fascination with wild animals. John Wesley tries to keep alive a young rabbit that he finds trapped in an abandoned well near his house, but fails. "He brought green things to it every day and dropped them in and then one day he fluttered a handful of garden lettuce down the hole and he remembered how some of the leaves fell across it and it didn't move. He went away and he could see for a long time the rabbit down in the bottom of the well among the rocks with the lettuce over it" (pp. 63–64). (McCarthy is no stranger to the principle of the one true sentence.) The boy also tries to nurse back to life a sparrow hawk he has found injured in the road. When it dies, he passes it off as a young chicken hawk and turns it in for bounty, then uses his dollar to buy traps that he sets out for muskrat and mink.

Warn has a pet buzzard that he flies on a string on windy days. "He cain't get up lessen they's some wind. So when we get a little wind I gen'ly fly him some" (p. 134). He and Boog hunt rabbits with Johnny's two dogs, which Boog calls "bugles." Warn tells John Wesley, while they sit by a fire Boog has built (by means of "a old Indian trick"), how Johnny had once caught a bullfrog in a mousetrap.

> He bet me a dope on it. I seen him come by the house with this mousetrap on a piece of bailin wire. Said he was fixin to catch him a bullfrog. We come on over and he set it on the end of that log there and then we went on to the store. I thought the poor bastard had done lost his rabbit-assed mind....
>
> Johnny Romines grinned. He told everybody in the store, he said.
>
> Yeah, we all like to of fell out laughin. So the son of a bitch bets me a dope he's caught one by the time we come back and sure as hell there he is. Pinched right by the ass. I like to never got over it. And wouldn't nothin do but we come straight back to the store frog trap and all and me buy him the dope right there. (pp. 136–37)

Warn traps a skunk in a small cave hole and crawls inside with him to shoot him. Johnny, his turn coming round, tells of a time when he and Warn wired an electric train transformer to a dynamite cap buried in snow beneath scattered bread crumbs and blew up a flock of hungry birds. "Lord," whispers Boog, "I'd like to have seen that" (p. 141).

The stories of Uncle Ather's they favor are all about "painters" and "wampus cats." Uncle Ather carries such a boyhood as theirs alive in his own memory and occasionally comes unstuck in time, loosened by some sudden intimacy with the natural world.

> In spring the mountain went violent green, billowing low under the sky. It never came slowly. One morning it would just suddenly be there and the air rank with the smell of it. The old man sniffed the rich earth odors, remembering other springs, other years. He wondered vaguely how people remembered smells.... Not like something you see. He could still remember the odor of muskrat castor and he hadn't smelled it for forty years. He could even remember the first time he had smelled that peculiar sweet odor; coming down Short Creek one morning a lot more years ago than forty, the cottonwoods white and cold-looking and the creek smoking. Early in the spring it was, toward the close of the trapping season, and he had caught an old bull rat with orange fur, the size of a housecat. The air

was thick with the scent of musk and had reminded him then of something else, but he could never think what. (pp. 56–57)

The novel's three narratives are linked by John Wesley's and the two adults' shared attachment to coonhounds, a special affinity that is significant in itself, since coonhounds are independent and solitary hunters as well as game dogs and the coon hunt therefore a ritualized contest between trained predator and prey, an ancient bridge between the human world and the feral one. Once, as readers, we are set into this environment, in which the human and not-human are so commingled—almost by definition alien to readers and to the act of reading—we are held there by the subliminal effect of metaphor. We are not allowed to forget how imperfect our assumed transcendence is, for in reading we are continually subjected to a simple and coherent stylistic code.

Marion Sylder's customized bootlegger's Ford, for instance, with compensatory weight shocks, once unloaded, is said to look "with its rear end high in the air like a cat in heat" (p. 165). A flashlight John Wesley drops, still lit, into the creek seems in the darkness "scuttling downstream over the bed of the creek like some incandescent water creature bent on escape"; his own hand as he reaches for it is like a "bat's shadow poised over the dome of light" (p. 100), before the flashlight inexplicably disappears as if sucked down into the river (though of course it has only gone out). A short time later, as his drenched body begins to thaw, his still frozen feet are "like hooves rattling inside his boots" (p. 104). When the sheriff and his constable come to old Ownby's house to arrest him for destroying government property, they turn back abruptly when he steps out armed to confront them at his front door and they can "see the mule ears of the old shotgun laid back viciously along the locks" (p. 185). Two sisters and their brothers, whom Marion Sylder and his sidekick, June, pass on the road at night, "caught in the yellow glare of the headlights [have] the temporarily immobilized look of wildlife, deer perhaps, frozen in attitudes of surprise predicating imminent flight" (p. 17). In the cave in which they briefly camp, John Wesley and his three friends come upon the signs of other dwellers. "They studied the inscriptions etched in the soft and curdcolored stone, hearts and names, archaic dates, crudely erotic hieroglyphs—the bulbed phallus and strange centipedal vulva of small boys' imaginations" (p. 139).

A list of such images is not, of course, literally inexhaustible, but the sense of the strangeness of the perceived world they convey certainly is. Such a list is worth making in the first place because even a brief one shows how persistently in the foreground McCarthy's subject is and how his constant reference from our world to the other causes the supposed autonomy of each to become highly problematical. McCarthy's figurative language is exact, and the metaphors therefore seem so inevitable that the effect is more one of the world's speaking through the writer than of the writer's speaking of the world. In turn, then, the world seems to draw even language into itself to lay claim to a prior authority.

Clearly enough we are not in a conventional grown-up children's narrative where the animals are simply human beings in appealing disguises, meant to be unthreatening and comprehensible. Arthur Ownby's uncharacteristically superstitious dread of cats is a pervasive reminder of this nature's patient claim upon us. Ownby is knowledgeable and self-sufficiently resourceful in the woods, where he thrives alone. He teases his friends at Eller's store, who are townies by comparison, for their not knowing the difference between a "painter's" cry and a hoot-owl's. But as he has grown older the cats have begun to trouble his dreams, "and he did not sleep well any more. He feared their coming in the night to suck his meager breath" (p. 59). He also believes that the cats may be possessed by the spirits of the dead, who have thus been taken back whence they came.

Awareness of his own impending death and recycling, regretted as the end of life as much as feared, is the source of these baleful fantasies.*

In these respects "Uncle Ather" is different from the boys, who at the innocent end of a life-span unreflectively fly buzzards on strings and catch bullfrogs with mousetraps. John Wesley is granted at least a premonition of what lies in wait, though it seems not to register on him, when a leech attaches itself to the bared leg of voluptuous and

---

*The welfare worker interviewing him in jail tries to determine his age, which he has difficulty remembering exactly. The agent says, "Well, could you tell us when you were born?" "If I knowed that," Arthur says patiently, "I could figure how old I was. And tell us that." "Well," says the agent, "could you estimate your age then? You are over sixty-five?" "Considerable," says Arthur. "Well, about how old would you say?" asks the agent. " 'It ain't about,' the old man said, 'it's either. Either eighty-three or eighty-four'" (pp. 219–20).

willing Wanita Tipton as she watches him seine for minnows—"a fat brown one just below her knee with a thin ribbon of blood going pink on the wetness of her skin"—thus complicating, and abruptly terminating, a potential sexual initiation.

Half of the Green Fly Inn, a local site of boisterous revelry, falls into the gorge it is precariously perched over (one corner of it is nailed to a pine tree) and joins the swept-out glass and refuse beneath it, collected to "a depth undetermined, creeping, growing, of indescribable variety and richness" (p. 13). A main part of the inn's specific charm has been its precarious station, its semblance to an old ship buffeted on dangerous seas. The hollow it is perched above acts as a flue for high winds, "funneling the updrafts from the valley through the mountain gap. . . . At times the whole building would career madly to one side as though headlong into collapse" (p. 12). Not long after the porch in fact collapses, carrying astonished drunks with it, the remainder of the inn itself burns, fired by the screaming updraft from the valley, and glides flaming into the pit. "There it continued to burn, generating such heat that the hoard of glass beneath it ran molten and fused in a single sheet, shaped in ripples and flutings, encysted with crisp and blackened rubble, murrhined with bottlecaps. It is there yet, the last remnant of that landmark, flowing down the sharp fold of the valley like some imponderable archeological phenomenon" (p. 48).

In the neighborhood the inn's burning inspires a festive mood, what with the warmth of the fire and the salvaged moonshine to be passed around among onlookers. In the novel the fire is vividly depicted, lingered over, the occasion of a comic tour de force; but after we are well past it, it takes on a symbolic aspect, associated as it is— one more occasion—with the awareness of nature's elemental power to reclaim its paltry human protégés without motive or warning. The subtly parodic echoes of an *ubi sunt* theme in the closing lines of the passage just cited force this connection upon us long before we know why.

John Wesley's pious mother believes God is punishing the patrons of the Green Fly for their sinning ways, but it is clear that she is only trying to impose a homespun theodicy upon an otherwise fortuitous and even comical event. In any case, even this wind is not so ill that it blows no one some good, for her cunning husband profits from the disaster: he relieves the men injured in the first collapse of their wallets and makes off into the night—and in fact uses that money to leave home. This unexpected complication of the Green Fly episode illustrates one of the difficulties in reading McCarthy: different functions of a given episode—merely descriptive, faintly metaphoric, and narrative—are presented with a carefully controlled parity, as if the means of threading our way through existence were itself as elusively unclear.

The fate of the Green Fly is a paradigm only if we make it into one, and we are encouraged to do that only by oblique —and spread-out— connections. One of the last of these is the most explicit. John Wesley's father, Kenneth Rattner, is killed by Marion Sylder, and his body is dumped into the disused insecticide-spray tank of the abandoned orchard (which Arthur Ownby "keeps"). The body remains there throughout the seven-year time span of the novel, gradually decomposing. Because of Arthur Ownby's eventually ritualistic visits to the pit we are afforded glimpses of it at random intervals. The last one comes in a passage abruptly juxtaposed with a description of the inmates on the grounds of the asylum to which Ownby has been sent. "The mountain road brick-red of dust laced with lizard tracks, coming up through the peach orchard, hot, windless, cloistral in a silence of no birds save one vulture hung in the smokeblue void of the sunless mountainside, rocking on the high updrafts, and the road turning and gated with bullbriers waxed and green, and the green cadaver grin sealed in the murky waters of the peach pit, slimegreen skull with newts coiled in the eyesockets and wig of moss" (p. 224).

The Jacobean luridness of this passage is not its only point. From the strictly human point of view the image, though overwrought, is supposed to be one of horror, inspiring revulsion. But the guidelines of *The Orchard Keeper* are not quite that simple. Since nature in *The Orchard Keeper* has claims upon our respect as well as upon our mortality, which in the Jacobean-Christian mode it clearly does not, one must think of the skull, though it requires a strain, as if it were an accommodation. From the newt's point of view that is precisely what it is, and all that it is, and the same could be said for the otherwise gothic trappings of the slime and the moss. Nature lives, without bias, off what comes to hand. Rattner's cadaver seems to mean something to Arthur Ownby, who oddly tends it; but to us, though it has an obtrusive symbolic aura, it is not finally and independently symbolic of anything. In the end it is simply recycled in a systematic, impersonal, ecological process, which, though it affronts our pretensions to transcendence, is not at all mysterious. In order to create a tension between what we habitually think and what we *should* think, McCarthy rigs this image so that it expresses simultaneously, in order that we see the difference, both the trite and the true.

In the late winter of this same year, in the novel's time, rain comes into the mountain and relentlessly stays, a rain so vast and unremitting that it threatens the wildlife and immobilizes humans. The streams flood and overrun their banks, stranding garfish to die eventually in cutoff pools. McCarthy's prolonged description of this phenomenon is precise and powerful, and the implacability of the force it represents is made to seem even more intimidating for its being so specific and impartial.

Toward the end of the period of this deluge, Marion Sylder, transporting moonshine, wheels up to Eller's store for gasoline. Inside, the two men exchange more or less good-natured and humorous insults, about paying bills and rich storekeepers and Eller's pathetic cat menagerie. Sylder then leaves, and the point of view switches from him to Eller—as if in *Ulysses* in "Wandering Rocks." This transition then conducts the narration in careful stages from an engagingly comic idiom into, once again, a portentously metaphorical one.

> The storekeeper drummed his nails on the marble ledge of the cash register for a minute. Then he turned and went back to his chair. He had been resting for only a short time when the clock among the canned goods began a laborious unwinding sound as if about to expire violently in a jangle of wheels and leaping springs, stopped, tolled off four doomlike gongs evocative of some oriental call to temple, then hushed altogether.
>
> Mr. Eller stirred from his chair, went to the clock and wound it with a key hanging down from a string. It made a loud ratcheting noise. Then he seized it from the shelf and slammed it back. It set up once more a low wooden ticking....
>
> Mr. Eller dozed and his head rocked in small increments down his shoulder, onto his chest. After a while a little girl in a thin and dirty dress came through the door behind the counter and gathered up all the kittens, now wailing louder and in broken chorus, carried them out again, talking to them in low remonstrances.
>
> Mr. Eller dozed, the clock ticked. The flypaper revolved in slow spirals. The wind had come up again and the rainwater blown from the trees pattered across the tin roof of the store, muffled and distant-sounding through the wallboard ceiling. (pp. 181–82)

Mr. Eller's down-to-earth nature, his snugness in his store and in his role in life, his unperturbed dozing while the cats wail and the rain drives on outside, are appealing, and seem meant to be. But it is also made clear that his sense of security in the grip of these elements is an innocence finally, as the clocks inside seem so curiously irrelevant, like complicated and inept mechanical toys, while real time, outside, prevails. We are being reminded, in relation to the novel's principal agenda, of the place of our identity in the impersonal scheme of things.

The Orchard Keeper has begun with a mysterious parable. Three men—two white, one black—are cutting a felled elm tree into lengths. They keep sawing into a length of iron fence that is somehow embedded in the tree's heart. They change angles and hit it again. Finally they give up. "It's growed all through the tree, the men said. We cain't cut no more on it. Damned old elum's bad enough on a saw. The Negro was nodding his head. Yessa, he said. It most sholy has growed all up in that tree." The characters and the location are not identified. For the time being the episode remains unassimilated. We can then only assume that some arcane metaphor is at hand and later on attempt to construe it. The fence that is supposed to have grown up into the tree, we assume in retrospect, has reference to the theme of man and nature interfused. In fact, the image is interesting in those terms because the fence that the baffled observers think has somehow grown into the tree—an odd instance of human vanity as well as ignorance—has of course been grown around by the tree, absorbed into it.

But the little story may be intended to have an altogether different relevance. Insofar as *The Orchard Keeper* is a merely human story, it is about the fencelike stubbornness and independence of the two men who are its central adult figures. Marion Sylder and Arthur Ownby are unlike each other except in these respects, and they are both models, in the end, for the boy who accrues an austere wisdom from his association with them. Sylder is a swaggering renegade, once a smuggler in Florida, now a whiskey-runner in Tennessee, part of a relay system from the source through Sevier County into Knoxville. He thrives upon taunting and thwarting the law. He drinks whiskey and chases women, drives fast new cars, is coddled by his wife.

Ownby, in contrast, is stately and shy of human company; he lives alone with his dog in a remote hollow, conversing only with the idlers at the store, which he infrequently walks to in order to trade for supplies, and with the boys who visit him to share his wine and hear his stories. He fills the balance of his old man's time savoring the nuances of the wilderness world he inhabits.

> From here he could see out into the valley, through the stark trees standing blackly in an ether of white like diffused mild, glazed and crystalline as shattered ice where the sun probed, the roofs thatched with snow, pale tendrils of smoke standing grayly in the still air.
> He could smell smoke, but he didn't think about it until it occurred to him that it had a sharp and pungent quality about it and he realized that it was cedar burning—postwood, not firewood—elusive in the cold air, in his nostrils, faintly antiseptic. (p. 157)

Perhaps for this reason he seems at times only recently to have evolved into the human state. Most of the wonderfully exact and rich descriptive sections in the book are presented from Ownby's point of view, expressions of his patient attention to and knowledge of his chosen world. He has, however, tried the conventional human way and failed at it. Through his scraps of memory we piece together a story of a younger Arthur, who took a bride, over the protest of her father, and was eventually rejected by her in favor of a traveling Bible salesman. (He still bears the scars from having been shot when he went to fetch her back.) This accounts for both his isolation and the air of sadness even in his peace.

The strong contrast between Ownby and Sylder is registered in two isolated sexual episodes, each typical of its participant. Sylder and his buddy, June Tipton, one night on the way to collect a load of whiskey pick up two girls and their brother and eventually pair off with the wary girls to cheerfully "needle" them, as one of the girls puts it, in a Negro churchyard—one pair in the outhouse, the other in the church itself. The girl June Tipton goes with had wet her pants moments before, and that and the logistics of copulating in the outhouse eventually becomes the subject of insensitive mirth. Later in the novel this episode makes a kind of off-rhyme with Ownby's recollections from his own past. He is remembering being himself of the age that John Wesley and his friends are now.

> Years back on summer nights he used to walk with neighbor boys two miles to the store to buy candy and cigars. They would come back over the warm and deserted roads talking and smoking the cigars. One night taking a shortcut they passed a house and saw through one window a woman undressing for bed. The others had gone back for a second look but he would not go and they laughed at him. The old man remembered it now with dim regret, and remembered such nights when the air was warm as a breath and the moon no dead thing. (p. 89)

The passage suggests that it is partly Ownby's generosity of heart that isolates him from others—those unlike him in this respect, such as Marion Sylder—but it also evokes a more fundamental loneliness that Ownby's meditative presence keeps alive in the novel down to its last page.

Marion Sylder's and Arthur Ownby's stories are linked more by theme than by common attributes or plot. That theme is the conviction each has that one should be able to live as one chooses—so long as harm is not done to others—independent of society's conventions and expectations. Each is also motivated by a strong sense of natural justice that serves as a code of dignity and honor. Each is an "anomic type" in these respects, but each is also scrupulously obedient to a responsible inner voice and an ordered inner world. Sylder, for example, has no compunction about slipping into the bedroom of Jefferson Gifford, the constable, and striking him in the face as he sleeps, because Gifford is a bully and has tried to frighten John Wesley into betraying Sylder. Later Sylder is beaten in jail by Gifford. When John Wesley comes to visit Sylder, he persuades the boy not to pursue the vendetta. The books, he says, have been balanced.

> Yes, he said. I busted him and he busted me. That's fair, ain't it?
> The boy was still silent, calmly incredulous.
> No, Sylder went on, I ain't forgettin about jail. You think because he arrested me that thows it off again I reckon? I don't. It's his job. It's what he gets paid for. To arrest people that break the law. And I didn't jest break the law, I made a livin at it. He leaned forward and looked the boy in the face. More money in three hours than a workin man makes in a week. Why is that? Because it's harder work? No, because a man who makes a livin doin somethin that has to get him in jail sooner or later has to be paid for the jail, has to be paid in advance not jest for his time breakin the law but for the time he has to build when he gets caught at it. So I been paid. Gifford's been paid. Nobody owes nobody. If it wadn't for Gifford, the law, I wouldn't of had the job I had blockadin and if it wadn't for me blockadin, Gifford wouldn't of had his job arrestin blockaders. Now who owes who? (pp. 213–14)

The argument is one that Ownby could appreciate: checks and balances, something keeping everything square, a kind of moral ecology. It is true that Sylder cannot make himself really believe what, for the sake of the boy, he pretends to believe. But his special hatred toward Gifford is the exception that, in its way, proves the rule, for though Gifford does not steal from greed or murder in anger, "he sells his own neighbors out for money"; and by Sylder's code this is worse. The law and therefore its agents are in conflict with value. This same point is made in Ownby's story, when his dog is shot by the county humane officer for no other reason than that, Ownby having been arrested, he is now a stray. The two men have this factor in common as well—besides, that is, the shared code and the relation to John Wesley: they get caught. The law prevails.

Between the two men and the boy there emerges what might be called a ghost community, complementary traits cohering around common beliefs. But the hypothetical community remains only an unfocused image, since community is not what any one of them is much interested in and since, in fact, Sylder and Ownby never meet. Their lives intersect in odd ways. Ownby from a distance sees Sylder one night loading whiskey. Sylder from a distance watches Ownby methodically firing his shotgun into the mysterious government tank, and he later thinks of this inexplicable circumstance as a portent of disaster for himself, suggesting a psychic communion or that their destinies have somehow got mixed up. It is the man Sylder killed whose remains Ownby tends, year after year, in the insecticide pit, though neither man ever knows of this connection either. And of course it is John Wesley's father who is in the pit, though the boy does not know that he is there and Sylder and Ownby do not know that he was the boy's father.

This odd and thought-provoking contrivance enables McCarthy to emphasize the disconnection of these people's lives, by showing from an aerial perspective connections that they at their level cannot possibly see. Again the experience of reading is manipulated, forced into play. We become ironic metaphysicians making order out of random data, though that order is as meaningless, finally, as the incoherence it supersedes: what ought to be or might have been is never a serious issue in this novel.

It is also true that Sylder and Ownby between them form a surrogate paternity for John Wesley, who has been abandoned by his father, a man who was never much of a father for him in the first place. (McCarthy's novels are overrun with dead, rejected, and absconding fathers.) John Wesley's mother, lost in her pious, irrelevant dreams, having made a glamorous myth of her pathetic fate, pays little attention to the boy and seems barely conscious of his comings and goings. He is parentless, in effect; and while this might cause another novelist's young hero to seem poignantly exposed, John Wesley is freed by it to become resourcefully solitary. Sylder adopts him, in his way, after John Wesley pulls Sylder from his car, which has been wrecked in the creek. (John Wesley also rescues Sylder's coonhound Lady from the creek.) Sylder gives him a coonhound pup and then keeps it for him when John Wesley's mother forbids him to bring it home. This relationship is the least original and least interesting aspect of the book, and McCarthy wisely does not make much of it.

The bonding between the two older men and the boy is less a main concern of the novel than a recognizable frame within which the other, less plotlike events take place. At the end the boy visits Sylder in jail and then Ownby in the state hospital and hears their stories and is moved by some primal instinct of identification to go to the courthouse and retrieve the sparrow hawk he had turned in for bounty months earlier. When he learns that instead of keeping the hawks for some worthy purpose the county has instead burned them, he is shocked and indignant.

> Burn em? he said. They burn em?
> I believe so, she said.
> He looked about him vaguely, back to her, still not leaning on or touching the counter. And thow people in jail and beat up on em.
> What? she said, leaning forward.
> And old men in the crazy house.
> Son, I'm busy, now if there was anything else you wanted . . .
> He smoothed the dollar in his hand again, made a few tentative thrusts, pushed it finally across the counter to her. Here, he said. It's okay. I cain't take no dollar. I made a mistake, he wadn't for sale. (p. 233)

By his ordinary standards, this for John Wesley is a major address, a measure of the clarity of the revelation that has fallen upon him—hence his symbolic gesture at the end, balancing the books, as Sylder might, and showing his colors. He has become conscious. For the three narratives this much closure has been achieved.

Even to talk about plots and closure in *The Orchard Keeper*, however, is to run the risk of distorting its character by throwing too great an emphasis upon the merely human aspect. The plots here are as spare as one would expect of plots built around characters who shun human society, rarely talk, and barely think—who are more-or-less committed on principle, in other words, to avoiding plot material. The plots are brought to them from the outer world, which itself may be said to be made up of plots (hence, for example, the deputy sheriff Earl Legwater's obsessed determination to salvage the piece of platinum that was supposed to have been implanted in Kenneth Rattner's skull). In the moral environment of *The Orchard Keeper* aimlessness is a virtue because it is only the aimless who can be adequately open to the saving rhythm of experience.

The authority of this rhythm is as definite in *The Orchard Keeper* as plots are in most novels, the basis of its structure. It is felt keenly in the alternation from Ownby in his age and instinctive attunement to his impending dying to John Wesley as a boy for whom the world is unfolding in a mystery that seems perpetual and unconfined. The fact that the two are so akin temperamentally causes them to remain mirror images that embody in human form the simple nature of the novel's world. In the last half of the novel this emphasis is distributed into the extended, vivid presentation of the snow and then the rain, the snow thickening and enchanting the austere landscape, the rain then ravaging and washing it away.

> Some time after midnight on the twenty-first of December it began to snow. By morning in the gray spectral light of a brief and obscure winter sun the fields lay dead-white and touched with a phosphorous glow as if producing illumination of themselves, and the snow was still wisping down thickly, veiling the trees beyond the creek and the mountain itself, falling softly, and softly, faintly sounding in the immense white silence.
>
> On that morning the old man rose early and stared long out at the little valley. Nothing moved. The snow fell ceaselessly. When he pushed the screendoor it dragged heavily in the drifts packed on the porch and against the house. He stood there in his shirtsleeves watching the great wafers of snow list and slide, dodging the posts at the corner of the house....
>
> The trees were all encased in ice, limbless-looking where their black trunks rose in aureoles of lace, bright seafans shimmering in the wind and tinkling with an endless bell-like sound, a carillon in miniature, and glittering shards of ice falling in sporadic hail everywhere through the woods and marking the snow with incomprehensible runes. (pp. 131–37)

> Still the rain, eating at the roads, cutting gullies on the hills till they ran red and livid as open wounds. The creek came up into the fields, a river of mud questing among the honeysuckles. Fenceposts like the soldiers of Pharaoh marched from sight into the flooded draws....
>
> ... Along Little River the flats stood weed-deep in livercolored water flecked with thatches of small driftwood and foam that coiled and spun near imperceptibly, or rocked with the wind-riffles passing under them. By day flocks of rails gathered. A pair of bitterns stalked with gimlet eyes the fertile shallows. At night the tidelands rang with peepers, with frogs gruffly choral. Great scaly gars from the river invaded the flats, fierce and

primitive of aspect, long beaks full of teeth, ancient fishes survived unchanged from mesozoic fens, their yellowed boneless skeletons graced the cracked clay-beds later in the season where the water left them to what querulous harridans, fishcrow or buzzard, might come to glean their frames, the smelly marvel of small boys.

    Rafts of leaves descended the flowage of Henderson Valley Road, clear water wrinkling over the black asphalt. The mud-choked gullies ran thick with water of a violent red, roiling heavily, pounding in the gutters with great belching sounds. (pp. 173-74)

The contrast between the two sections is not uniform or naïvely schematic, but the prevailing mood in each case, interrupted at intervals by aspects of the other, is strongly in the foreground—exquisite elemental beauty, exhilaration, and warm camaraderie balanced against an almost formal desolation and loneliness: "From a light-wire overhead, dangling head downward and hollowed to the weight of ashened feathers and fluted bones, a small owl hung in an attitude of forlorn exhortation, its wizened talons locked about the single strand of wire. It stared down from dark and empty sockets, penduluming softly in the bitter wind" (p. 143). The effect of such passages is important because it heightens our awareness of the mysterious bonding and separation of the human and non-human, of a first rhythm of life that is antecedent to thinking and structures.

    Ownby is in charge of this theme of the narrative because he is old enough to know and to respect the world's dialectical law. When he discovers Kenneth Rattner's body in the pit, his first reaction is revulsion and indignation—since it has invaded his orchard—but his almost immediate response afterwards is, curiously but characteristically for this aspect of the narrative, both practical and ritualistic. He cuts a small cedar tree and drops it into the pit across the body. Thereafter, once a year, in the yuletide season, for nine years, he adds a new sapling to the concealment. The strategy is sensible and resourceful: the invasion of his solitude by the corpse itself would be nothing compared to what would ensue if others were to come to know of it. The distinctive odor of the cut cedar also masks the odor of corrupting flesh, an effect that in turn buffers the persistent thought of death itself in the old man's mind. He is a sturdy survivor not only in the respect that he has remained alive, against the odds, but in the respect that he chooses to live, quietly affirming existence not only with the pattern of his life but also with each act in it. His resourceful seasonal ritual cannot be spoken of accurately as a symbol of anything so grandiose as life out of death. The point is both simpler and more profound: it affirms being alive as opposed to being dead. Ownby's ritual is an act of choice that is informed by knowledge.

The two children who actually discover the corpse and point Ownby to it can only flee, being properly terrified by this gaping apparition that they cannot hope to understand. They have been picking berries when they encounter the thing, and when they leave their berry pails behind, like pathetic signs of something lost forever, Ownby calls out after them, "Hey! I got your berry buckets, . . ." (p. 54); but they have disappeared without a trace, as if they have fled into the children's story where they properly belong.

Ownby's standing there alone holding the berry pails of the children whom he has tried to befriend is only one of many occasions in which his presence in the narrative draws us toward its other, more desolate, theme. His own solitude is chosen; but it is also continuous, as he seems instinctively to know, with the ultimate solitude of dwelling in an ungregarious universe, lost, as it were, in the stars. We are kept mindful of this, subliminally, by the way in which our perspective on Ownby keeps changing, from intimate association with his perceptions and feelings to an abstracting distance from him.

> The old man carried out the last of his things and piled them on the sledge, buckled them down with the harness straps he had nailed under the sides. He went back in one more time and looked around. Some last thing he could save. He came out at length with a small hooked rug, shook the dust from it and put it over the top of the sledge. He took up the rope and pulled the sledge to the road and called for Scout. The old dog came from under the porch, peering with blue rheumy eyes at his indistinct world of shapes. The old man called again and the dog started for the road, hobbling stiffly, and they set out together, south along the road, until they were faint and pale shapes in the rain. (p. 188)

It is made to seem a cruel order of things that cannot permit this agreeable, enduring old man, with his reverence for life, to fill up the world as he, like anyone else, must assume that he does. On the day he is apprehended he has come down from his last refuge in the mountains, unsuspecting, to trade his ginseng root at the store. He is conscious of all of the detail of where he is as he moves along, absorbed in the complex abundance of the new spring.

> Crossing the slide they entered the deep woods once more, the sun winnowed in tall fans among the spiring trunks, greengold and black vermiculated on the forest floor. With his cane the old man felled regiments of Indian Pipe, poked the green puffballs to see the smoke erupt in a poisonous verdant cloud. The woods were damp with the early morning and now and again he could hear the swish of a limb where a squirrel jumped and the beaded patter of water-drops in the leaves. Twice they flushed mountain pheasants, Scout sidestepping nervously as they roared up out of the laurel. (p. 200)

But a government agent waits for him at the store, and suddenly it is all over for Ownby, more quickly and finally than he could imagine.

> The old man had stopped. He was looking at the man, and then he was looking past him, eyes milk-blue and serene, studying the dipping passage of a dove, and beyond, across the canted fields of grass to the green mountain, and to the thin blue peaks rising into the distant sky with no crestline of shape or color to stop them, ascending forever. (p. 202)

He sees in this instant the vacant, unimplicated space that he has always inhabited and is now, worst of all, absent from.

In the mental hospital to which Ownby is assigned he is unhappy because being amidst so many people seems an incongruity to him. But, of course, they are even more alone than he.

> The brick buildings atop the hill are dark with age, formidable yet sad, like old fortress ruins. Families come from the reception room into the pale sun, moving slowly, talking, grieving their silent griefs. The unvisited amble hurriedly about the grounds like questing setters, gesticulant and aimless.
>
> There are others who sit quietly and unattended in the grass watching serene and childlike with serious eyes. Tender voices caress their ears endlessly and they are beyond sorrow. Some wave hopefully to the passing cars of picnickers and bathers. The eldest of all sits a little apart, a grass stem revolving between his yellowed teeth, remembering in the summer. (pp. 223–24)

This passage directly precedes the one, cited earlier, presenting the last image of Kenneth Rattner's skull, with the algae and moss growing on it and the newts obliviously making their home within. Death is only the ultimate form of isolation, the living spirit no longer there to confuse the issue.

Many years later, John Wesley returns from an unexplained exile, now motherless and fatherless and with vivid but scattered memories of his childhood and of the old man. He visits his mother's grave, thinking that its lettering—MILDRED YEARWOOD RATTNER—somehow gives her importance, "like having your name in the paper" (p. 245). And for a moment a curiously inconsequential scene takes precedence over everything else that might have crowded into this epilogue. John Wesley is sitting in the cemetery near a traffic light. A car stops at the light, and the woman in it looks at John Wesley. She turns to the man driving, and they both look. John Wesley waves to them, but neither waves back. The light changes, and the car moves on, the woman looking at him still, the man looking ahead. John Wesley waves again, the woman still watches without waving, and the car slides away. The scene is moving because we sense a dim kinship to John Wesley's mother and father in those watching, unresponding faces. But it also reminds us of the inmates on the lawn at old Ownby's final home waving hopefully to the cars of picnickers and bathers as they pass, striving naïvely to bridge the unbridgeable separation in human lives.

We also learn with a shock of temporal displacement that the elm tree being sawed up in the beginning of the novel has in fact been felled here, in this cemetery, on this very day, when John Wesley has returned to visit his mother's grave: "The workers had gone, leaving behind their wood-dust and chips, the white face of the stump pooling the last light out of the gathering dusk." The iron fence embedded in the tree is the fence that encloses the cemetery. It marks off the living from the dead; and when the tree is taken down, a torn gap remains in it, leaving us with yet another disconcerting sign. John Wesley walks through this gap when he leaves, headed toward the western road, as the rain "mizzles softly" (p. 246); and in that western prospect nature is being permitted, for our readerly edification, one last episode of display behavior, a spectacle the very grandness of which is made from the day's death and its submission to the night: "the darkening headlands drawing off the day, heraldic, pennoned in flame, the fleeing minions scattering their shadows in the wake of the sun."

With all of these stops being pulled out at the end, one might expect McCarthy's young hero to succumb to thematic stress, but not so. During most of this he is abstractedly sitting on a gravestone with one shoe off, testing his sock for wetness, and whistling softly to himself. The point is a nicely wholesome and incongruous one, about how memory and an assured inner life overcome the sedition of dread. John Wesley has touched his mother's gravestone, and the experience is meaningless to him. He feels only that "a carved stone [is] less real than the smell of woodsmoke or the taste of an old man's wine. And he no longer cared to tell which were things done and which dreamt."

II Word and Flesh
Outer Dark

In major respects *Outer Dark* is a mirror image of *The Orchard Keeper*, and a corresponding change has taken place in the values expressed. Recessive themes of *The Orchard Keeper* have been made to dominate. *The Orchard Keeper*'s elusive and affecting aura of loneliness and disconnection has been made to prevail and become an insistent theme in *Outer Dark*. A corollary difference is that whereas in McCarthy's first novel the main characters were stubbornly identified with their setting, in *Outer Dark* they are uprooted wanderers at best inhabiting an obscure, existential void. In *The Orchard Keeper* the sense of being located is meticulously conveyed; a good deal is made of signposts, of measured distances from one place to the next, of maplike spatial relationships. In *Outer Dark* the topography is vague, dreamlike, and surreal in a way that imposes an unwholesome, deranged aspect upon the entire scene. The distances are all walking distances, and the time span covered cannot be more than a few months; but within those limits the characters encounter bafflingly incongruous aspects of landscape—sluggish rivers, mountains, moss-laden trees, swamps, precipitous gorges. This, of course, reinforces our sense of the characters as utterly dislocated and homeless not only in their negotiated space but in the world as well. At this level *Outer Dark* is a disturbing, powerful representation of not being at home in the world, of the perceived, scary disconnection of the human from the not-human that both Freud and Heidegger called the *unheimlich*.

Since the narrative structure is also naïve—more rigorously controlled than in *The Orchard Keeper* but therefore less dense—the dreamlike setting and pace bring an almost medieval aura of allegory to the events; but that allegory we find to be so successfully encoded that our approach to meaning is at once invited and thwarted. This experience in turn gives us a sense of what it is like to be the searching but unreflective characters we are reading about. In *Outer Dark* the world is given back the terror that in *The Orchard Keeper* had been held at bay (the corpse concealed by the evergreen tree in the spray pit in this respect seems emblematic), and we with our stabilizing capacity for moral reasoning are as displaced from that world (and as threatened by it, intellectually) as the characters in it are displaced spatially and in every other way. The embodiment of evil in *Outer Dark* is both convincing and inexplicable, of human form but resistant to being human, beyond and opposed to civilization. In *Outer Dark* McCarthy shows best his remarkable capacity for unlearning all that he knows, for unraveling history itself, in order to reperceive and render the world in a primitive, unrationalized form. He reminds us, as Freud did, that what we know, though it gives a reason and order to what we fear, does not therefore also extinguish what we fear or even seriously incapacitate it in the long run.

The two principal characters of *Outer Dark* wander about as if in a maze that has no center to it or exit. The analogous condition in the novel is that of blindness, repeatedly invoked by allusion or by direct reference, mostly by demented preachers. In this particular world of McCarthy's these are, metaphorically, definitive states. The two characters, brother and sister, alter egos in effect, are each homeless and helpless. The gothic dispensation remains enfranchised and unmitigated throughout. *Outer Dark*, in short, is as brutally nihilistic as any serious novel written in this century in this unnihilistic country. Faulkner's influence upon McCarthy is pervasive, and *Outer Dark* is conducted audaciously in (or perhaps as) the very shadow of *Light in August*; but McCarthy is, if anything, even less sentimental about deliverance than Faulkner was. McCarthy's Lena Grove, Rinthy Holme, remains in her maze and has no ingenuous acolyte attending; and her child, rather than being proof against the world, is proof of it.

Yet, as forbidding and uncompromising as *Outer Dark* is, as untouched by wishful thinking, it is a beautiful book as well—chaste, shapely, and compassionate—and this unlikely combination of intrinsic and extrinsic factors finally makes a statement in itself, any paraphrase of which will seem inadequate. McCarthy's skill as a presenter of scene and his strange trust in the principle of eidetic rendering can cause mere discourse to seem both superfluous and inexact.

The blind man whom Culla encounters in the novel's last section claims to be doing the Lord's work but denies that he is a preacher: "No. No preacher. What is they to preach? It's all plain enough. Word and flesh. I don't hold much with preachin" (p. 240). Introduced as it is, after all of the novel's main events have taken place, the blind man's laconic theology seems less Christian than Manichaean, for the separation of word and flesh in *Outer Dark* is complete; and the word is, moreover, decidedly unmanifest, an alien idea. "They's lots of people on the road these days," Culla has said, and the blind man has agreed: "I pass em ever day, people goin up and down in the world like dogs. As if they wasn't a home nowheres." The blind man's faith is both unrationalized and "blind" in that it has no reference to experience of the world, but the man knows what is lacking from the world and therefore what ought to be there, or somewhere, whether it is or not.

Homeless wandering in *Outer Dark* is a metaphor for everyone's state. Within this state a version of word-and-flesh dualism is apparent in the separate stories of Rinthy and Culla—not the same as word and flesh but akin to it, for Rinthy believes and envisions, whereas Culla, demoralized and displaced by his own guilt, is without hope, feeling, motive, or direction. He is a being without desire, whose milieu is shadow, negation, and death. Circumstances, moreover, tend to confirm *his* conception of the world rather than Rinthy's, just as the blind man, Culla notices—for all his inner vision—is making a slow progress into a swamp. The darkness, as the title implies, appears to be encompassing, that which is outside our dream of the world—that is, that which is real.

Rinthy, in search of her child, who has been taken from her by Culla at birth, is followed everywhere on her journey by small lights from one source or another. Culla's story is conducted mostly in darkness. Rinthy is trusting, virginal—in all respects except the one—and driven by an idealized love; she is taken in and cared for wherever she goes, by women and men alike. Culla, who is motivated at first only by guilt (he has conceived the child by Rinthy and then, in shame for that, left it to die), is repeatedly derided, set upon, and driven out—shown simple justice at best—and is finally offered a sinister facsimile of friendship, an insinuated blood brotherhood, by a trio of night riders who phlegmatically murder and pillage, leaving behind them, for Culla to negotiate, an evil, circumambient wake.

Rinthy and Culla each inhabit a world that the other cannot be aware of and that each to some extent makes. This division remains purposefully absolute. A union is anticipated but never realized. Once they are separated, these imperfect representatives of word and flesh never again meet. Their paths cross—they pass through the same towns and encounter some of the same people (though this has to be "ciphered" by us, since the people act differently in their different presences)—but their journeys are conducted otherwise in lonely isolation, as if their kinship were an aberration and their separation were natural. It is conceivable that Culla longs for Rinthy in some way, since he knows her well enough to know that without her he is dreadfully incomplete. He tells people he is looking for her, but nothing else he does would indicate that. He tells the night riders at the end that if they can together find Rinthy, she will take the child and care for him; however, they kill the child anyway—which, in effect, is what Culla himself earlier had tried to do. But since to our view Culla has virtually no thoughts, he has no thoughts of Rinthy that we are privy to. This may be an opaque effect of the ambivalence he expresses in his actions, a kind of internal canceling out. He stays in motion, but he is also totally paralyzed.

The world that Culla moves around in displays the same eerie inertness that Culla himself does, persuading us in a different way that it is he who is normative and Rinthy who is the discontinuous exception. An oppressive air of purposeless waiting, like humidity, prevails throughout the novel. The torpid, circular pacing of dialogue and action is scrupulously regulated by McCarthy to deepen this effect, and otherwise unrelated images are spaced throughout the text to implicate in the setting a whole nature of impeded being. Corpses are dug up and robbed of their clothes and left on view this way in a town that is not much more than a dusty corpse itself. Culla is constantly seeing himself in the form of his own shadow. Bodies of hanged men seem suspended at random everywhere, visible and inert. An angry squire is struck from behind with a brush hook and folds in half mechanically, as if hinged. Culla is told the story of a mink trapper who dies from snakebite and is found locked in rigor mortis "kneelin down like somebody fixin to pray. Stiff as a locust post.... They said they had to break ever bone in his body to get him laid out in his box. Coroner took a sixpound maul to him" (p. 120). A family riding into town sitting in chairs on the wagon are said to seem like "stone figures quarried from the architecture of an older time" (p. 77). The eventual fate of the tinker for whom Rinthy searches is similarly paradigmatic, a condensation of these other hinted meanings, as he hangs, an inert center for an impersonal, inflicted process.

> The tinker in his burial tree was a wonder to the birds. The vultures that came by day to nose with their hooked beaks among his buttons and pockets like outrageous pets soon left him naked of his rags and flesh alike. Black mandrake sprang beneath the tree as it will where the seed of the hanged falls and in spring a new branch pierced his breast and flowered in a green boutonniere perennial beneath his yellow grin. He took the sparse winter snows upon what thatch of hair still clung to his dried skull and hunters that passed that way never chanced to see him brooding among his barren limbs. Until wind had tolled the tinker's bones and seasons loosed them one by one to the ground below and alone his bleached and weathered brisket hung in that lonesome wood like a bone birdcage. (p. 238)

Culla is repeatedly required to negotiate or fend off thick vegetation, weeds, waist-high grass, encroaching stands of trees. He is identified with such masses as Rinthy is, more sentimentally, with birds, butterflies, moths, and changing light. When he spits into the stream he is frantically trying to cross in the dark—after abandoning the baby—his flare of saliva inexplicably moves upstream. At the end he comes to another appropriate dead end at another swamp, its "naked trees in attitudes of agony and dimly hominoid like figures in a landscape of the damned" (p. 242). He is followed everywhere by silence.

> Holme wiped his mouth on his naked arm and tried to swallow and then went on chewing. It was very quiet. He listened but he could hear no sound anywhere in the woods or along the river. Not of owl or nightbird or distant hounds. (p. 175)

In this instance Culla is participating, unwillingly, in an evil communion with the night riders around their campfire. What he is having difficulty chewing and swallowing is an unidentified sinewy meat, conceivably human. He has got to this place on a ferry whose cable-rigging has broken loose in the swollen river, killing the ferryman and another rider and leaving Culla drifting in both darkness and a silence that seems to suck sound into it.

> He could hear the whisper of water going up and down over the deck. It sounded as if it were looking for him. After a while he cupped his hands and hallooed into the night. There was not even an echo. His voice fell from his mouth in a chopped bark and he did not call again. He wondered how far away the shore could be, and the dawn. (p. 167)

When Culla comes across the three men for the last time, he has limped out of the woods into a small field, "insects rising out of the dark and breaking on his face like rain and his fingers trailing in the tops of the wet sedge," and he can hear no sound "save a faint moaning like the wind but there was no wind" (p. 231). Once, earlier, the trio have passed him in the night.

> Something had passed on the road and he lay huddled against the chill of pending dawn with his arms crossed on his chest in that attitude the living inflict upon the dead and he listened but he could hear nothing. There was something fearful about. He listened for dogs to bark down along the road but no dogs barked. He lay awake a long time and the morning came up in the east in a pale accretion of light heralded by no cock, no waking birds. (pp. 145–46)

When swamp peepers hush as he approaches and then recommence after he has passed, he is said to move "in a void claustral to sound" (p. 131). Culla's world is an eerie stasis, the people in it exhibiting only a joyless stoicism. It is a vacancy and a silence, and his wordless wandering is only an extension of it in another form. Dreamlike and oppressive, his rural landscape with its blank, unsettled spaces has become the image of an inexplicable emptiness and loss. McCarthy seems most concerned to deny the world of the grids of understanding we habitually impose upon it—ethical, psychoanalytical, cultural—in order to force us to renew our acquaintance with it as, in this case, an incoherent and unrationalized gestalt of mass and process, without design or purpose, unless it is that some demented and unapproachable God invisibly presides.

In such a context Culla's passivity in fact seems like a resigned obedience to an inexplicable and unmanipulable destiny. His blind counselor, who may indeed, as in a dream, be a displacement of himself, says, "What needs a man to see his way when he's sent there anyhow?" (p. 241). Sight and will are thus equated; and Culla's part of the story, in association with the outcome of Rinthy's—one guided by volition but to an inconceivable tragic end—seems to bear out the message. Culla appears to believe that he has set his destiny in motion by conceiving the child with Rinthy.

His story in fact begins with a dream in which he is set upon by an angry mob for causing the sun to go out. A healing prophet, foreseeing an eclipse, has told the assembled "delegation of human ruin" (p. 5) that the sun will go dark and then return and they will all be healed, including the dreamer himself, who, though not blind, diseased, or lame, has begged to be cured too. But when the sun does not pass through the eclipse and the darkness stays, the crowd turns upon him, the dreamer, rather than the prophet; and he is awakened by Rinthy, who has been awakened by his crying out, into a "night more dolorous" even than that of the dream. From the dream, we infer Culla's guilt and his despair of being "cured" of it, and we see that, like a curse that he has brought upon the world, he now has remade the world in his own blighted image. The dream creates the world in which the sufferers suffer, and he is doomed to be the victim of other people's mysterious displacements. He is like a character from Kafka in that his somewhat puny existence is wholly determined by forces that are unseen and unpredictable. "What needs a man to see his way when he is sent there anyhow?" Culla appears to have punished himself by giving up, and everyone else's guilt has become his own. He has managed to have himself cast out from a tiny place that he ruled absolutely into a world in which he is absolutely ruled.

He is accused by one of several squires he works for of being a fleeing felon, simply because he cannot otherwise account for himself. In a town called Cheatham he is imagined to be a grave robber and is pursued because he is an outsider and behaves guiltily. Later he is almost shot but instead is brought to a crude country justice by the man who owns an abandoned, dilapidated cabin Culla innocently sleeps in for one night and whose outrage is absurdly out of proportion to the nature of Culla's crime. He is accused by witless brothers and an itinerant preacher of spooking a vast drove of hogs and thus of causing the death of the brother whom he has just before engaged in friendly, aimless conversation. In his experience, swift transitions from the relaxed jousting of male country humor to sudden breathtaking violence are normal, as if a separate aspect of his punishment were to live each day an entire spectrum of human existence, like some generic character from *The Divine Comedy*.

Culla seems or has made himself to be almost wholly without needs. He takes each instant as it comes upon him, never projecting into a future, dwelling in a moving pocket of time. It cannot be said, then, that he is punished for overweening pride or that he brings any of the particular misfortunes upon himself. He is quite sane and clearheaded compared with the ones who victimize him. He is taken advantage of simply because he has no station in life and no position of moral strength to fight from. Eventually there is hardly any significant difference, ontologically, between his dream life and the real world; either world for the bourgeois reader is an existential nightmare.

This particular aspect is vividly realized toward the end in two episodes. One is the occasion of sheer terror aboard a suddenly pilotless ferry, with Culla trapped there, free falling, so to speak, through darkness, on a racing river with a savagely terrified horse that he cannot see. The other, his coming upon an abandoned house, not long after the ferry incident, is a gothic parody—like a newly discovered Grimms' tale—of coming home.

> It was a very old cabin and the ceiling of the room he stood in was little higher than his head, the unhewn beams smoked a foggy and depthless black and trellised with cobwebbing of the same color. The floor was buckled and the walls seemed tottering and he could see nothing plane or plumb anywhere. There was a small window mortised crookedly into the logs of one wall, the sash hung with leather hinges. That and the long clayless chinks among the logs let in the waning light of this day and wind crossed the room with the steady cool pull of running water. There was a claymortared fireplace of flatless and illfitted fieldstone which bulged outward in the room with incipient collapse, a wagon spring for lintel, the hearth of poured mud hard and polished as stone. A serpentine poker. Two wooden bedsteads with tickings of husks and a halfbed with a mattress on which lay curled a dead cat leering with eyeless grimace, a caved and maggoty shape that gave off a faint dry putrescence above the reek of aged smoke. He took hold of the mattress and pulled it from the bed and dragged it to the door, fighting it through the narrow opening and outside and long bright red beetles coming constantly from beneath the cat to scatter in radial symmetry outward and drop audibly to the floor. He threw the mattress in the yard and went back in. In the kitchen a doorless woodstove propped in the front with two bricks against the floor's fierce incline. A partitioned mealbin with sifter and a hard dry crust of meal adhering to the wood, the meal impregnated with worms whose shed husks littered the floor of the bin among micedroppings and dead beetles. A solid butternut safe in which languished some pieces of cheap white crockery, chipped and handleshorn coffeecups, plates serrated about their perimeters as though bitten in maniacal hunger, a tin percolator in which an inverted salmoncan sat for a lid. A nameless gray dust lay over everything. (pp. 195–96)

Culla's surname of course has "home" hidden in it, but he cannot spell it and has never seen it spelled. We learn this as he is being arraigned by John, unhappy owner of the abandoned house, before the squire. When he is treated decently by this shrewd and self-contented man—sentenced to ten days' labor on his place, working off a five-dollar fine—Culla's response is to wish to stay even longer.

> What for?
> Well, just to stay. To work.
> At fifty cents a day?
> I don't care.
> Don't care?
> I'll stay on just for board if you can use me.
> It was very quiet in the kitchen. The squire was standing with one hand on the door. The woman had stopped her puttering with dishes and pots. They were watching him.
> I don't believe I can use ye, Holme, the squire said. Holler when ye get done. (pp. 207–208)

It is a point at which we realize how young Culla is, after all, and that his exile is absolute, that he has no place to be.

The spectral magi treat Culla as an apprentice member of their group. They are associated with him constantly by spatial proximity—as if he dreamed them up too. Their leader says, pointedly, "We ain't hard to find. Oncet you've found us" (p. 233). Culla is often suspected of the atrocities they commit. They too are headed nowhere in particular: "From nowheres nowhere bound." The leader wears boots he has forced Culla to give him, which Culla himself had stolen from the first squire who had helped him; Culla wears what is left of the boots of the nameless and mute imbecile of the group. It is from Culla's boot that the leader draws the knife with which he slits the child's throat.

That he actually kills the baby Culla himself had left to die in the beginning suggests that the difference between them is one of degree rather than kind, and in this case a matter even of style. They not only are bound nowhere but are bound, as the leader sardonically says, "by nothin." They are beyond even the most elementary taboos. They kill without compunction or motivation. They live and feed without distaste off whatever comes to hand. The leader wears a black suit taken from a disinterred corpse. The imbecilic one eagerly drinks the blood from the throat of the killed child. They are the ultimate, if not the logical, extension of the "anomic type."

What is at stake in the cryptic exchanges between Culla and these smugly grotesque outlaws is the simple, premetaphysical issue of human identity. The leader mocks Culla's sullen tenseness: "never figured nothin, never had nothin, never was nothin. . . . [Culla] was looking at nothing at all." Our gaze is shifted to the mute and nameless one who "seemed to sleep, crouched at the man's right with his arms dangling between his knees like something waiting to be wakened and fed."

>What are you? Holme muttered.
>What?
>He said it again, sullenly.
>The bearded one smiled. Ah he said. Now. We've heard that before, ain't we?
>You ain't nothin to me.
>But the man didn't seem to hear. He nodded as if spoken to by other voices. He didn't look at Holme.
>You never did say what you done with your sister.
>I never done nothin with her.
>Where's she at?
>I don't know. She run off.
>You done told that.
>It ain't nothin to you. (p. 234)

"You ain't no different from the rest," the leader says finally. "From any man borned and raised and have his own and die they ain't one man in three got even a black suit to die in."

The leader seems to regard himself as the philosopher of an opportunistic and obliterating nihilism. Names, for instance, he says in several different ways, are wholly arbitrary fictions, providing the namers with the illusion of having known and claimed a part of the world and the named with the illusion of being somehow significantly human. But "names dies," he says, "with the namers. A dead man's dog ain't got a name." All of this is distilled to its essence when Culla asks to be given the child, saying feebly, "You don't need him"; and the leader replies, "Water in the summer and fire in the winter is all the need I need. We ain't talkin about what I need ... that ain't what's concerned." That he is without needs identifies the leader with Culla and also makes him, by his own reckoning, generic, the true and unacknowledged essence of the human world, the ultimate reduction of the human—what we all are, he is claiming, under the skin, beyond our frivolous dreams and prayers. He slits the nameless child's throat to make his point, and the otherwise human child at that instant becomes merely food, like a slaughtered pig.

The blind man at the end seems to be addressing himself to this same issue, countering the leader's cynicism in effect by enshrouding it in mystery. He has asked Culla if there is anything he needs. Culla says,

> Need?
> Anything you need.
> I don't need nothin.
> I always like to ast.
> What are ye sellin?
> I ain't sellin nothin. I'm at the Lord's work. He don't need your money.
> It's good he don't need mine. I reckon you're some kind of a preacher.
> No. No preacher. What is they to preach? It's all plain enough. Word and flesh. I don't hold much with preachin.
> Holme smiled. What have you got to give? Old blind man like you astin folks what they need.
> I don't know. Nobody's never said.
> Well how would you expect to get it?
> Just pray for it.
> You always get what you pray for?
> Yes. I reckon. I wouldn't pray for what wasn't needful. Would you?
> (p. 240)

Culla admits that he has never prayed, thus, in a sense, putting himself outside the blind man's frame of reference.

The point of this juxtaposition in the novel is not that one of the instructors is right about the nature of reality and the other wrong but that the two positions put together in this unprecise way make a kind of koan, and a koan that can't be right or wrong. The blind man's question, "Is there anything you need," might itself be called a psuedo koan, since it is a question that contains its own answer—that what one needs for "salvation," existential or religious, is need itself, the established determinant of the human. The blind man going around asking this question is "doing the Lord's work." Both of Culla's instructors allude, presumably without knowing it, to a plainer statement of the problem, by King Lear, in a larger text that is no less ambiguously nihilistic than the one at hand:

> O reason not the need! Our basest beggars
> Are in the poorest things superfluous.
> Allow not nature more than nature needs,
> Man's life's cheap as a beast's.

To the extent that we need, in this special sense, we are human; to the extent that we do not, we are people "going up and down in the world like dogs." The one man of the evil trio with a name, Harmon, is said to be like a "lean and dirty cat" (p. 175). The leader himself originally wears a boot that is cleft like a hoof. Culla and the friendly hog drover engage in a comical discussion about whether hogs that have uncleft hooves like mules' are truly hogs (they conclude that a hog is a hog), and this seems in the end to allude obliquely to the subject of what a human being is. The friendly drover goes over the cliff with the panicked hogs, and so does Culla eventually, escaping the drover's dimwitted confederates. When he looks back from the river, they seem against the pale sky "like small, erect, simian shapes"; and in his last glimpse of them they are moving along the bluff "with no order rank or valence to anything in the shapen world" (p. 227). When Culla parts from the blind man and heads on down the road, he goes "soundless with his naked feet, shambling, gracelorn, down out of the peaceful mazy fields, his toed tracks soft in the dust among the cratered shapes of horse and mule hoofs" his shadow in the high sun be-wandering "in a dark parody of his progress" (pp. 241–42). The blessed human form of William Blake's imagination undergoes such transmogrifications repeatedly in *Outer Dark*. Even when Rinthy finally finds her child, without realizing it, he is no more than some bones and a tiny "calcined ribcage" (p. 237).

The impoverishment of the inhabitants of *Outer Dark* is authentic—that is, economic, not simply a smart literary device. But impoverishment is also a state of being that permeates the environment. Culla does not pray because he has learned to be—except for weak moments—without desire; and if he and his kind are lost in any sense, it is partly on this account. In this text, being "gracelorn" in either the secular or the Christian sense comes essentially to the same thing.

By the idea of grace we are brought back from Culla's swamp—where even the trees have "dimly hominoid" shapes and rise from a "dead land where nothing moved save windy rifts of ash"—to Rinthy. It is difficult for us to imagine that any association with her, even incestuous, could be evil, because she is so wanting—so enchanted and compelled by her need. Culla has brought her licorice candy from the store. All she desires at first from the tinker is cocoa, which he does not carry, though he does sell whiskey and lewd books. The tinker is identified by her only as the one "they said never had no cocoa" (p. 55); and the storekeepers do not have cocoa either.

Culla's separation from her—morally and then spatially—is fatal to his identity. She in turn never sees her child—except in his final, lowest-common-denominator form—but her dream of finding him is unimpaired by realities, and it sustains her through her brave and pathetic quest. Until her time runs out she is protected in two ways by her ignorance: she has only a vague, intuitive sense of the evil forces dispersed around her, and this innocence and vulnerability in turn touches a kindly empathy in those whom she encounters and who therefore wish to take her in rather than—as with Culla—turning her away. Her mere presence seems expected to bring good fortune, as if she embodied a charm, grace in some form. The isolation that she lives in from the start (knowing no one in the world but Culla, not knowing which way town is, having nowhere to run off from or run off to) causes her in the first place to seem to inhabit some existential void—prior to data and consciousness—which she fills, as our own sparse paradigm, by going around, as she puts it, hunting her chap: "That's about all I do anymore," she says (p. 156).

But that isolation suggests also how discontinuous she is from the world around her and how incompatible her nature is with the world she passes through. She is absurd in that her idea of the world is better than the one that is. In her reticent and modest way she is defiant and heroic, but she is also dead wrong. At one point she passes the spot where two innocent men have been hanged. She almost fails to see them ("if crows had not risen from a field she might never have looked that way" [p. 100]); but when she does, she stands "for a moment watching them, clutching the bundle of clothes, wondering at such dark work in the noon of day while all about sang summer birds. She went on, walking softly. Once she looked back. Nothing moved in that bleak tree" (p. 100). Later she admits to a cranky old woman (who despises snakes and varmints of all kinds) that she is scared sometimes, being alone. "I always was scared. Even when they wasn't nobody bein murdered nowheres" (p. 116). What she is talking about is not, however, the difference between the way things actually were before and are now but the difference that she now *knows* about, which is the same thing for her as what is.

Rinthy's estrangement is not metaphysical but a simpler estrangement of the senses: she seems to have been born full-grown into the world without having time to learn how to appropriate and humanize it. Her innocence, in other words, creates the paradoxical effects of causing her to be trusting and hopeful, on the one hand, and uneasy and threatened, on the other, by all that she sees and hears.

> They rode on through the new green woods under the rising sun where wakerobins marked the roadway with their foiled wax spears, climbing,

the man jiggling the reins across the mule's tattered withers, through a cutback and into brief sunlight where the old woman hooked her bonnet more forward on her head and peered sideways at the others like a cowled mandrill, her puckerstrung mouth working the snuff that lay in her lower lip, turning again, a jet of black spittle lancing without trajectory across the edge of the wagon and into the woods, descending, the man working the brake, the wagon creaking and sidling a little in loose gravel, onto the flatland again, fording a weedgrown branch where dead water rusted the stones and through a canebrake where myriad small birds flitted and rustled dryly like locusts.

She watched the wet wheeltracks behind them go from black to nothing in the sand, caressing the rolled shift in her lap. It's a likely place for varmints such a place as this, ain't it? she said.

The woman looked about them. Likely enough, she said. (pp. 67–68)

Rinthy's outward experience is a dialectical churning of incompatible elements, signs of beauty and peace intermixed with signs of violence and menace, like the hanged men among the singing summer birds. The decent old woman resembles a "cowled mandrill" because years ago she lost her nose when a stovepipe she was lifting fell and sliced it off. Yet she is kindly, the matriarch of a kindly, if laconic, family that has taken Rinthy in. Just moments before, her odd role as a focusing point has been crystallized for us by a touching, simple gesture:

The old woman had turned her chair partly sideways and rode peering into the passing wall of wet shrubbery as if she held camera with something that paced them in the black pine woods beyond. After a while she leaned precariously from the wagon bed and broke a small twig from a spicewood bush, held it to her nostrils a moment and then with her opaque orange thumbnail began to fray the end of it. (p. 67)

Such recurring incongruities, never simple and never thematically assertive, compose a world that is textured with mystery, one that will not lay itself plainly before us as a moral design. Insofar as Rinthy is at the center of it, the conflicting signals show the points of contact between her inner and outer life, the crossover phases from a subjective to an objective reality that is threatening *because* it is objective, or other. As her experience, this pattern is particularly evident in the long, beautiful passage, cited in the introduction, that takes Rinthy from washing up at the family's house to going to bed, an episode in which the ordinariness and the strangeness of the world come together as in some rustic hierophantic epiphany. Meaningfulness emanates even where there is no meaning.

This dialectical pattern shows on the larger scale of the novel in the scheme that alternates episodes of Rinthy's story in her world with episodes of Culla's in his, with the occasional surrealistic intrusion of the night riders in small intercalary chapters. It is shown too in the difference between Rinthy as she sets out to find her child and as she ends up. She is like this in the beginning:

> She went about the house gathering her things, laying out her dress on the bed and examining it before she stripped out of the shift and put it on. She pirouetted slowly in the center of the room like a doll unwinding for just a moment and then took off the dress and scrubbed herself with a rag and cold water as best she could and with a piece of broken comb raked her dead yellow hair. She set out her shoes and dusted them and put them on, and the dress. Of the shift she made a package in which lay rolled her small and derelict possessions and thus equipped she took a final look about to see what had been forgotten. There was nothing. She tucked the package beneath her arm and set forth, shortgaited and stiffly, humming softly to herself and so into the sunshine that washed fitfully with the spring wind over the glade, turning her face up to the sky and bestowing upon it a smile all bland and burdenless as a child's. (p. 53)

But she is like this at the end:

> Late in the afternoon she entered the glade, coming down a footpath where narrow cart tracks had crushed the weeds and through the wood, half wild and haggard in her shapeless sundrained cerements, yet delicate as any fallow doe, and so into the clearing to stand cradled in a grail of jade and windy light, slender and trembling and pale with wandlike hands to speak the boneless shapes attending her.
> And stepping softly with her air of blooded ruin about the glade in a frail agony of grace she trailed her rags through dust and ashes, circling the dead fire, the charred billets and chalk bones, the little calcined ribcage. She poked among the burnt remains of the tinker's traps, the blackened pans confused among the rubble, the lantern with its skewed glass, the axle and iron wheelhoops already rusting. She went among this charnel curiously. She did not know what to make of it. She waited, but no one returned. (p. 237)

The beauty of Rinthy's belief in her child is all but mathematical in its purity and in its relation to the empirical world. In the beginning, because of this, she is identified with light, simply, as with the sunlight in the first of the two passages here. But that identification becomes progressively more ambiguous and ironic as her status in the world does—and as her hopes become frayed.

When she is taken in by the friendly family, she is first seen by them and sees them in lamplight from deep darkness: "She was met at the door of this small house by a man holding aloft a lantern beyond which and gathered in its fringe of wan light she could see the faces of several women of different ages, including an ancient crone who was without a nose" (p. 57). When she goes out to the pump that night to wash up, she bears the lamp "votively" before her with its heat "rising pleasantly about her face." "She watched the ground, going with care, the basin upright and riding her hip, slowly, processional, a lone acolyte passing across the barren yard, face seized in the light she bore" (pp. 62–63). She meets the son in the family on her way back. He emerges from the darkness, the sky "heavy and starless above them," to say, absurdly, "Kindly a pretty evening, ain't it?" (p. 64). The boy tries to tease her into blowing out the lamp to prove that she is not afraid of the dark, but she refuses and moves on into the house "with her air of staid and canonical propriety," leaving him standing there in the dark. This seems plain enough, if even intended metaphorically: the world as darkness encompassing Rinthy's composed, subjective, and attracting inner light. But earlier in the evening, when the lamplight was cast upon her, it also cast a shadow, rendering her for a moment with the surreal morbidness of a symbolist painting: "They watched her sit, holding the bundle up before her, the lamp just at her elbow belabored by a moth whose dark shape cast upon her face appeared captive within the delicate skull, the thin and roselit bone, like something kept in a china mask" (p. 59).

Soon after this she sleeps throughout a night alone under a bridge even through the first light, "gently washed with river fog" (p. 97). When she does rise, she washes and then emerges from beneath the bridge to set forth. "Emaciate and blinking and with the wind among her rags she looked like something replevied by grim miracle from the ground and sent with tattered windings and halt corporeality into the agony of sunlight. Butterflies attended her and birds dusting in the road did not fly up when she passed. She hummed to herself as she went some child's song from an old dead time" (pp. 97–98). *Replevied*, a legal term, seems like merely fancy diction in this context; but it is also, characteristically for McCarthy, strikingly exact and suggestive, since it refers to property being restored provisionally to the original owner by a contesting one. The song from a dead time is, we guess, a dead time of hers and thus ominously out of touch with the real present. An "agony" of sunlight is markedly different from sunlight as a sentimental benediction, and complex as well, suggesting suddenness, struggle, and pain.

In the next town that Rinthy comes to she is compelled to see a doctor because of her swollen, still lactating breasts. Her embarrassed obliqueness together with the doctor's quiet and patient kindness make this incident a marvel of understated human eloquence. Yet for the entire time that Rinthy waits in the plain office the light around her, because of an impending rain storm, grows progressively dimmer. "It was very quiet in the room. The light waxed and waned ... the room was growing darker. A gust of damp air moved upon them.... She could hear the rain outside and it was dark enough to want a lamp.... The room was almost dark and they could hear the steady small slicing on the glass and the spat of it on the stone sill" (pp. 152–53). This darkness is a gloomy darkness at a time when Rinthy is being cared for and reassured, and so it casts an indefinable sadness across the small, touching episode, underscoring the hopelessness of Rinthy's situation even as she is wild with hope. The world's ways and human ways remain at unmediated cross-purposes. The lawyer who leads Rinthy to the doctor has already made a point of this by saying, "We get a lot of rain here in the fall.... After it's too late to do anything any good" (p. 151).

Rinthy finds her tinker, but he refuses to yield up the child. He threatens her and then leaves her weeping. He hears her keening "a long way down the road," and suddenly she is extraordinarily transformed in the prose, as if in a pagan myth, by an ambitious reach of metaphor. "He could hear it far over the cold and smoking fields of autumn, his pans knelling in the night like buoys on some dim and barren coast, and he could hear it fading and hear it die lost as the cry of seabirds in the vast and salt black solitudes they keep" (p. 194). After this Rinthy lives briefly with an unidentified farmer. When we see her here, she is mute and wooden. And she is sitting in a rocker, not rocking, on the porch of the house in full darkness. The flowers in the dooryard have curled and drawn "as if poisoned by dark" (p. 209). The man has to bear the lamp for her to lead her to the kitchen at supper. She is unresponsive to him; he is downcast in anger and sorrow. Rather than quarrel, or speak even, she leaves to go to bed, fading "from the reach of the powdery lamplight." The man thinks of his work. Then: "A moth had got in and floundered at the lamp chimney with great eyed wings, lay prostrate and quivering on the greasy oilcloth tablecover. He crushed it with his fist and flicked it from sight and sat before the empty plate drumming his fingers in the mothshaped swatch of glinting dust it left" (p. 211).

When Rinthy comes at last to the place of her child's death, "half wild and haggard in her sundrained cerements" (p. 237)—the "agony of sunlight" echoing forward—it is into a glade that she walks, as Culla at night had done before her, there to come upon the evil men who murder the child. The word *glade* is direct kin to the word *glad*, and both are related etymologically by a common source denoting brightness or light. Such an irony is so cruel as almost to violate a decorum between author and character, but it is there and deliberately so. Rinthy picks her way through the charnel of the fire, and not knowing what to make of it she simply waits. "She waited all through the blue twilight and into the dark. Bats came and went. Wind stirred the ashes and the tinker in his tree turned slowly but no one returned. Shadows grew cold across the wood and night rang down upon these lonely figures and after a while little sister was sleeping" (pp. 237–38).

Rinthy herself has lived daily with the cruelest irony of her story. Her belief in her idea of her child, though it provides a deliverance for her—from a vacant, purposeless life—also causes her breasts to swell and to lactate, bringing her continual pain. She is too simple to know how to release her own milk or even that she can or should. Homes that she comes to and could stay in she has to leave finally because of literally painful reminders of her state. In one home there is a new baby, left there to be tended, and Rinthy leaves without explanation. In another there are mounds of fresh butter newly made by the bitter and weary woman of the house—"Don't need sorry," she says, "not in this house. Sorry laid the hearth here. Sorry ways and sorry people and heavensent grief and heartache to make you pine for your death" (p. 105). All of the mocking surfeit of manna is destroyed in an alarming fight between the woman and her shiftless husband as Rinthy flees in fear. But then in the very next house she is taken into there sleeps an old sow who is said to have eaten all of her "hoggets" save one. Rinthy is accused by the sow's owner of having herself killed her own offspring—"bagged it for the river trade" (p. 112). Rinthy's love and her pain are inseparable. This causes her discontinuity with the world she moves through to seem unbridgeable; her pain is *caused* by her choice to love and need, by her unwillingness to be less than human.

The grim poignancy of the symbol, to Rinthy, of her milk and of her faith in the life of her child (the doctor she sees does not dissuade her from this conviction) owes partly to its being in contrast with the facts. The child is alive, but he is not the child Rinthy imagines. In fact, in these terms he is Culla's child more than Rinthy's, an issue of sin and guilt rather than of love.

> He looked at the child. It had a healed burn all down one side of it and the skin was papery and wrinkled like an old man's. It was naked and half coated with dust so that it seemed lightly furred and when it turned to look up at him he saw one eyeless and angry red socket like a stokehole to a brain in flames. He looked away. (pp. 231–32)

The child by this point has passed through progressive stages of evil custody—from Culla to the tinker and now from the tinker to these three evil revenants of darkness, as they are called, willfully subhuman. Culla has believed, or pretended to, that the child was "puny" from birth, not likely to live; to Rinthy he has sounded not "puny" but "peart," but she of course never sees him and never has control over his pitiful destiny.

The tinker who steals the child seems to want him as a recompense for the rejected and loveless life he has had to lead.

> I give a lifetime wanderin in a country where I was despised. Can you give that? I give forty years strapped in front of a cart like a mule till I couldn't stand straight to be hanged. I've not got soul one in this world save a old halfcrazy sister that nobody never would have like they never would me. I been rocked and shot at and whipped and kicked and dogbit from one end of this state to the other and you cain't pay that back. You ain't got nothin to pay it with. Them accounts is in blood and they ain't nothin in this world to pay em out with. (pp. 192–93)

He appears to think of the child as a charm and, ironically, even as a new start for himself and the world: "I've seen the meanness of humans till I don't know why God aint put out the sun and gone away," he says, repeating the image of Culla's first dream. But when it occurs to him during his encounter with Rinthy that the child might be Culla's, the product of sin and incest rather than an emblem of innocence, even this feeble hope is blighted; and he leaves Rinthy in vengeful anger, taking the child with him nevertheless. In that the real child is without a name, uncared for, adrift, without significance, and eventually only an object, and then meat, he is our grimmest analogue in this novel's world; and only Rinthy's love, hopelessly naïve and powerless, is like what we might imagine God's to be.

When Rinthy enters the glade at the end, she is said to stand in the clearing "cradled in a grail of jade and windy light" and to step softly in a "frail agony of grace" (p. 237). In that same cradle and grail are the remains of a fire containing, with the other charred bits and pieces of the tinker's possessions, the bones and surviving rib cage of her child. The phrase *agony of grace* is the right one for her because it precisely describes her bravely oxymoronic status in the world, which now has driven her mad. She is the human dream of the world still alive in it, if barely. We are perhaps being asked to believe—and allowed to by the pervasive symbolist aura of the text—that her only true home is in words, a paradoxical extension of her wordless innocence, and that in a world as bereft of God, or at least of grace, as this one of McCarthy's there is no other place for her to be.

III The Ambiguities of Innocence
Child of God

The strangeness of the story of Lester Ballard, the child of God, begins not with its subject matter but with the way the story is told. Even by McCarthy's ordinary standards, an unusual degree of unassimilated raw material impedes—or seems to impede—the central narrative flow. We are nearly halfway through the novel before the shocking main theme of the story—Lester's necrophilia—is securely under way; and even from that point forward, when the narrative focus is much sharper, the material of the story itself is not much more than would flesh out a long short story. Before that point the narrative is so aimless and fragmented that an innocent reader might wonder if there is even to be a plot.

Stories about Lester are related to us by unidentified narrators speaking at times to unidentified friends, and these stories as often as not lead to other stories that are not related to Lester at all. The course of Lester's life in the first half of the novel is random and directionless, guided by no plan or principle of motivation: Lester goes to buy a jar of moonshine whiskey from Fred Kirby, who can't remember where his stash is hidden; Lester comes across a car at night with a couple obliviously humping away inside, is spied, and runs away; Lester's appropriated shack is invaded by foxhounds; Lester pays a visit to Reubel, the dumpkeeper, and ogles his sluttish daughters; Lester goes to church and snuffles loudly through the service, vexing the congregation; Lester tries to shoot a fat bass in the creek; Lester explores an abandoned quarry; Lester encounters a drunken whore in the woods, jerks her nightgown off, and gets beat up, by the whore, and put in jail; Lester goes to the carnival and wins three stuffed animals before he is run off; Lester watches from a hill as boarhounds pursue, attack, and kill a wild boar; Lester gets shown how to dress an axe; Lester catches a frozen robin and takes it as a gift to a moronic baby in the house of a sullen girl he is attempting to court. Then

Lester comes across a couple asphyxiated in a still-running car, and the story suddenly takes form.

Meanwhile there are the stories about Lester and the spin-offs from them: about how he beat up a smaller kid who wouldn't retrieve a softball from the briers; about the time he broke a stubborn cow's neck by trying to pull the cow off its spot with a rope tied to a tractor; about a sick bird dog named Suzie; about a con man at a fair who pretended to shoot (with a rifle) released pigeons that were actually blown up by implanted firecrackers; about one storyteller's unlucky fight, at another carnival, with an ape; about someone named Old Gresham singing the chickenshit blues at his wife's funeral; and then about how Lester's father had died.

> I don't know. They say he never was right after his daddy killed hisself. They was just the one boy. The mother had run off, I don't know where to nor who with. Me and Cecil Edwards was the ones cut him down. He come in the store and told it like you'd tell it was rainin out. We went up there and walked in the barn and I seen his feet hangin. We just cut him down, let him fall in the floor. Just like cuttin down meat. He stood there and watched, never said nothin. He was about nine or ten year old at the time. The old man's eyes was run out on stems like a crawfish and his tongue blacker'n a chow dog's. I wisht if a man wanted to hang hisself he'd do it with poison or somethin so folks wouldn't have to see such a thing as that. (p. 21)

Since it is clear that all of the stories told about Lester are being told at some point after the events of the novel have taken place, it is also clear that Lester has become a part of the mythology of his region and has thereby achieved, ironically, a place in the community that has eluded him otherwise. Moreover, since the narration has been so scrupulously decentralized from the beginning, it seems intended to be as much about the place and the people in it as about Lester himself. By these two means Lester becomes something like the spirit of the place, a bizarre aberration certainly, but not so totally dissociated from the people of that place that he doesn't seem somehow like their collective nightmare.

The community of Sevier County, Lester's habitat, is presented in the novel as being all but pathologically placid. No distress is shown to evoke anxiety or to disturb the calm surface of tested structure and polite social amenity. Yet it is made to seem possible that if the community were reconstructed by some inexpert, godlike hand, with some of the wires connected to the wrong terminals, a Lester Ballard might result. The normalness of the community contains a conventional disposition toward violence, ritualized in hunting and fighting, and a preoccupation with death and with the dead, expressed in favored, repeated stories; and its very atmosphere seems charged with sexual energy. Lester has all of these same wires, but he is wired differently, so he turns out dangerously wrong, an aberration and a norm at the same time, an unconscious being brought forth, as if by sorcery, into the conscious world. And he is saved in the end for our mercy not only because he is like us in a perverse form but because he retains to the end, by some kind of incomprehensible courage—overcoming more abasement than most humans could imagine, much less bear—the capacity to judge himself. His simple version of Kurtz's melodramatic "The horror! The horror!" at the end of *Heart of Darkness* is to return to the hospital from which he has, in effect, escaped and to say to the nurse attending, "I'm supposed to be here" (p. 192).

Lester and his story are freakish and sensational, but they are worth attending because McCarthy has conceived pathetic Lester as a berserk version of fundamental aspects of ourselves—of our fear of time, our programmed infatuation with death, our loneliness, our threatening appetites, our narcissistic isolation from the world and the reality of other people. The story is told in such a way as to impose incoherence upon coherence, coherence upon incoherence; it reproduces in itself the irregular and obscure countermovements of existence—of thinking, feeling, and acting—that cause form and meaning to separate and fly apart. Ironically, Lester is most deadly once he has a vision of his life and imposes a form upon it and in so doing achieves a mirrored inversion of what communities are supposed to do and be. Moreover his own order brings to the novel the shape that it has been waiting for, an aesthetic contour that is mocked by the materials it is made of. Lester makes his life with a story in a novel that is partly *about* stories and storytelling and thus passes over the edge from fact into fiction, where behavior is no longer required to be restrained—any more than stories are—by taboo.

McCarthy does not obtusely confuse the normal with the abnormal as if saying that there is no difference under the skin between Lester and his neighbors. The difference is vast; and it is made to seem, if anything, even more so by an exaggeration of the normal, as if going on in life as though nothing in the world is wrong with it is, for the citizens of Sevier County, an unimpeachable article of faith. The exaggerated stories of real atrocities and real violence are safely buffered by the ritualistic, good-old-boy context in which they are told. On one occasion a point is made of this when a man in a group telling Lester stories offers to tell another—"Talkin about Lester..."— and one of the listeners replies, breaking it and the interlude off, "You all talk about him. I got supper waitin on me at the house" (p. 81).

Late in the novel, heavy rains cause the Little Pigeon River to overrun its banks and flood, to the tops of the parking meters, the entire city of Sevierville. The ordinarily disastrous situation is dealt with characteristically by being made a joke of. The high water becomes simply another aspect of the daily routine and is absorbed into the reassuring authority of the normal. The deputy, rowing in to the courthouse to pick up the sheriff, makes a joke about having given Bill Scruggs a ticket for "goin up Bruce Street speedin in a motorboat" (p. 161). Rowing up the main street, as on any other day, "past flooded shops and small cafes," the pair are greeted by friendly citizens.

> Mornin Sheriff, called out the man in the water, raising his hand.
> Mornin Ed, said the sheriff.
> The man in the boat gestured with his chin.
> Did Mr Parker see you? said the man in the water.
> We're just goin up there now.
> Seems like trouble ought to make people closer stead of some tryin to rob others.
> Some people you cain't do nothin with, the sheriff said.
> Ain't that the truth.
> They rowed on. Take care, said the sheriff.
> Right, said the man in the water. (pp. 161–62)

The sheriff and deputy inspect Eustis Parker's store, which has been broken into. Guns have been stolen. They row on to the post office to check the mail. On the way back to the courthouse they pick up another citizen and give him a ride. The citizen tells stories, as they go, about the old days. Allusions are made all the way through this episode to the flood as a judgment on the meanness of people—for which there is ever new and old evidence—but the talk about Noah and about the "good lord" desiring to rid himself of the town is presented as just country talk, acknowledging the meanness of people and moralizing by generalizing that too.

THE AMBIGUITIES OF INNOCENCE 57

> You think people was meaner then than they are now? the deputy said. The old man was looking out at the flooded town. No, he said. I don't. I think people are the same from the day God first made one. (p. 168)

The old man has been telling about the old days of the White Caps—proto-Klansmen of east Tennessee—supposedly vigilantes but in reality a "bunch of lowlife thieves and cowards and murderers." "People don't want to hear about that," the old man says, making an important point for the novel. And he tells one of the specific reasons why. The White Caps had been driven out finally by a legendary deputy. Two remnants convicted of murder in 1887 had been hung in 1889 on the courthouse lawn, the feature attraction of a festive community gathering ("I remember there was still holly boughs up and Christmas candles").

> People had started in to town the evenin before. Slept in their wagons, a lot of em. Rolled out blankets on the courthouse lawn. Wherever. You couldn't get a meal in town, folks lined up three deep. Women sellin sandwiches in the street. Tom Davis was sheriff by then. He brung em from the jail, had two preachers with em and had their wives on their arms and all. Just like they was goin to church. All of em got up there on the scaffold and they sung and everbody fell in singin with em. Men all holdin their hats. I was thirteen year old but I remember it like it was yesterday. Whole town and half of Sevier County singin I Need Thee Every Hour. Then the preacher said a prayer and the wives kissed their husbands goodbye and stepped down off the scaffold and turned around to watch and the preacher come down and it got real quiet. And then that trap kicked open from under em and down they dropped and hung there a jerkin and a kickin for I don't know, ten, fifteen minutes. Don't ever think hangin is quick and merciful. It ain't. But that was the end of White Cappin in Sevier County. People don't like to talk about it to this day. (pp. 167–68)

The flood can be taken in stride—it never really achieves an autonomous metaphorical status from the point of view of the novel; the meanness of people can be taken for granted. What is not open to community scrutiny, as the old man implies, is the ambiguity of the normal and what is covered over by the collective belief in it and the effort to sustain its placid and reassuring rhythm. It is worth repeating that no one in this community is even remotely like Lester; but the difference along the human spectrum is one of degree, not kind, and that difference is sustained by an almost apprehensive overcorrection, as if by some effect of collective auto-hypnosis.

The shrewdly interpolated episode of the flood ends with another story, which, partly because it is otherwise pointless, clearly *is* symbolic, alluding subtly to the subject at hand—the unfailing human capacity for suppression and evasion: "As they ascended the courthouse stairs he was telling them how an old hermit used to live out on House Mountain, a ragged gnome with kneelength hair who dressed in leaves and how people were used to going by his hole in the rocks and throwing in stones on a dare and calling to him to come out" (p. 168). The emblem of civil authority represented by the courthouse is a nicely incongruous effect here; the psychoanalytical space between the steps of the courthouse and the old hermit's cave on House Mountain is vast. The sheriff himself is an ambulatory version of the courthouse image—patient, forceful, and unflappable, heir to the legendary Tom Davis, scourge of the White Caps, a subliminal reminder of what it is that keeps us from becoming Lester.

Alert readers will hear, too, in the story of the crazy hermit—given the context of Lester's story—a sly allusion to the ur-limerick about the old hermit named Dave who kept a dead whore in his cave, a connection that implicates all who have laughed at the doggerel and passed it on. When later the posse goes searching aboveground for Lester in the woods at night, Lester is symbolically underneath them in his caves and darkness; and at that point he is no joke.

Lester's own story is another of McCarthy's meditations on the theme of homelessness, living in the unhomelike; and the permutations of Lester's status in relation to the domestic world are signs of what is taking place within him. His mother has deserted him, and his father has hung himself as a consequence. After his father's death Lester is literally dispossessed. His house and farm are put up for auction by the county and thereby taken from him. This event makes the first scene of the novel, and it is rich in irony. Like the hanging of the White Caps, the auction is a festive, almost Chaucerian, occasion for the townsfolk. ("They came like a caravan of carnival folk up through the swales of broomstraw and across the hill in the morning sun, the truck rocking and pitching in the ruts and the musicians on chairs in the truckbed teetering and tuning their instruments, the fat man with guitar grinning and gesturing to others, in a car behind and bending to give a note to the fiddler who turned a fiddlepeg and listened with a wrinkled face" [p. 3]). Lester is standing at the time in the dark barn where his father had hung himself, where in fact the severed rope still hangs. The auctioneer gives a long-winded but persuasive speech about land as an investment and, of all things, the sound future of property. Lester is hit in the head with an axe when he tries to prevent this invasion and appropriation of his property.

Then, rather than being taken in as a ward of the county, he is set adrift. He sets up with his own mattress and his rifle in an abandoned house, which he shares at different points with spiders, mosquitoes, a black snake, a pursued fox, and pursuing foxhounds. Hunters have stripped siding from the house, exposing it and Lester to the elements. Lester lies asleep in it "like a dead man" (p. 16). This house burns down in the first winter, when Lester overstokes the fireplace (he is oddly oblivious to the nature of the materials of which the world is made). The fire takes his first dead consort with it, consuming her without a trace. He moves into a cave with his salvaged rifle and mattress and, now, stuffed animals; after this move he commits his first murder and then the rest of them, uncounted, and populates his house beneath the normal world with dead female victims. When the cave is in danger of being discovered, he moves to a new one with even deeper reaches of caverns, transporting his entire retinue body by body through the rain and across mudslides and a swollen creek in a furious, demented achievement of heroic stamina. Wherever he goes, he takes his mattress, a solitary and forlorn link to the civilized state. He loses his toy bear in the flooded stream and with it the strange connection with what there is of a child left in him.

He has gone farther and farther from the world and deeper into madness. The complex nature of his madness seems perfectly expressed in the bizarre decor of his cave. The walls with their "softlooking convolutions" are "slavered over . . . with wet and bloodred mud" and have an "organic look to them, like the innards of some great beast"; the bodies of his victims, in contrast, are arranged on stylized pallets of stone, lying, incongruously, "like saints" (p. 135). Two such grotesquely incompatible modes of being have somehow merged in Lester's mind.

When Lester has thus reconstituted a family, he is moved by one more cruel homing instinct to reclaim his original dwelling. He begins to haunt his old house and to spy upon John Greer, who is now cozy there and whom Lester in his paranoia considers a threatening enemy. In a hopelessly deranged way Lester seems intent on making his way back. But he is now wearing the clothes of his victims and a wig fashioned from the scalp of one of them. He has ceased to be himself by becoming his victims, but he is still compelled to return home. The passion to return to his home is his undoing, for he is almost killed when his frantic attempt to kill John Greer fails. This last crime is the only incautious one Lester commits, and its very recklessness—it is obviously doomed to fail—is a sign of some profound desperation that his customary wary prudence cannot overcome.

Lester is hospitalized, under guard, because of his gunshot wound; and when he is taken from his room by a band of citizens who want to force him to lead them to the bodies of his victims, he is conducted through a garbled reenactment of the stages of his exile and alienation. As at the auction he is taken by force from the place where he eventually realizes he is supposed to be. The men stop at one man's house to get Lester warmer clothes, and home is momentarily revealed as if through a door opening into a different space: "A man left the car behind Ballard and went to the door. A woman let him in. Inside under the glare of the naked bulb he could see the woman and some children" (p. 179). He is made to put the clothes on and he notices that they are soft and smell of soap: he has only this brief experience of normal life.

But it is not long before he is deep within the caves again, having escaped his captors, this time in foreign territory with no mattress and a dying light. He is eventually alone in darkness, the bones and skulls of dead ancient animals around him, his own state imaged in an abyss that outreaches the beam of his light and the fall of stones. He imagines himself dying there in the final ironic horror of the unhomelike place, mice nesting and spawning young in his skull, centipedes sleeping in the "marrowed flutes" of his bones (p. 189). One small shaft of light breaks in from a crevice, and Lester patiently claws away stone and dirt toward that surface. When he finally emerges, what he sees first is like a mockery, a picture-book image of a tranquil rural scene: a cow grazing, beyond the cow a barn, beyond the barn a house. Lester has traversed an entire spectrum of being in one small place. He scrambles out, crosses the fields, reaches a road, and sets out on it in a direction, pointedly, away from the mountains. A church bus full of children passes him, lit up, and Lester sees looking out at him in the darkness—even though there is nothing to see—a boy who, he realizes, looks like he did as a boy, his lost self. It is after this that he returns to the hospital, saying only, "I'm supposed to be here," expressing in the statement both a judgment of himself and a forlorn, dim acknowledgment of an idea of home. Yet he ends up dying in what is referred to in the narration as a cage.

Through all the convolutions of his obsessed experience Lester remains the victim of an unlikely conflict of impulses. He cannot be understood as a wild man, strictly speaking, certainly not as bestial. He is beyond the pale both socially and psychoanalytically, and McCarthy offers nothing in the foreground that would explain him, has the good sense not to want to. But as aberrant as Lester progressively becomes, he is ruled at every turn both by unspeakable appetite and by a warped compulsion to domesticate it. The truly horrifying aspect of his ghoulish family is that it is less like an underground city of the dead than it is like a monstrous dollhouse where the corpses, along with his stuffed bears and tiger, become facsimile people, literally manipulated as their limbs grow stiff, arranged and rearranged.

> He went outside and looked in through the window at her lying naked before the fire. When he came back in he unbuckled his trousers and stepped out of them and laid next to her. He pulled the blanket over them. (p. 92)
>
> He sat and brushed her hair with the dimestore brush he'd bought. He undid the top of the lipstick and screwed it out and began to paint her lips.
>
> He would arrange her in different positions and go out and peer in the window at her. After a while he just sat holding her, his hands feeling her body under the new clothes. He undressed her very slowly, talking to her. Then he pulled off his trousers and lay next to her. He spread her loose thighs. You been wantin it, he told her. (pp. 102–103)

Events imply that deep at the core of the normal waits this child in us as well, insatiable, self-gratifying, and solipsistic. Lester has never achieved even elementary maturity and is therefore without discipline or taboo, has never passed over from the child's fictional world into the adult's world, where fact expresses itself in the otherness of other people. The dead woman for whom he has bought clothes he has also violated previously in the car in which he found her dead along with her boyfriend, the two of them asphyxiated while copulating. Lester has had to move the half-clothed body of the dead man out of the way in the back seat in order to get between the dead woman's legs. One of the man's eyes is still open, and his condom-sheathed penis is still erect. Lester has to stand on the dead man's legs to enter the woman, and he seems to do this without compunction.

Uninhibited by even the most basic taboo, Lester has passed into a state that is a parody of innocence, as his ramshackle squatter's house and his caves will become parodies of home, odd versions in turn of stability and arrested time. "Coming up the mountains through the blue winter twilight among great boulders and the ruins of giant trees prone in the forest he wondered at such upheaval. Disorder in the woods, trees down, new paths needed. Given charge Ballard would have made things more orderly in the woods and in men's souls" (p. 136).

To say that Lester commits crimes against nature is to say also that he is both at war with nature and oblivious to its reality. That he thinks he can suspend time is a sign of this peculiar innocence to begin with (the tableau of the first asphyxiated couple in the car seems to have somehow permanently warped his perception of time), though the eventual status of his cherished corpses should have been sufficient to dispel this illusion: "The bodies were covered with adipocere, a pale gray cheesy mold common to corpses in damp places, and scallops of light fungus grew along them as they do on logs rotting in the forest. The chamber was filled with a sour smell, a faint reek of ammonia" (p. 196).

Flux for him means only deprivation, the unraveling of a life, diminution. Various images accrue in the early stages of his exile to reinforce this partial truth. Coming out of an abandoned quarry he has explored, he hears a door banging, an "eerie sound in the empty wood.... He passed a rusty tin shed and beyond it a wooden tower. He looked up. High up on the tower a door creaked open and clapped shut. Ballard looked around. Sheets of roofing tin clattered and banged and a white dust was blowing off the barren yard by the quarry shed" (p. 39). A stray dog has followed him here. When he calls, the dog is gone. The nine daughters of his friend the dumpkeeper one by one run away and disappear. A black man he meets in jail, being held to be hung for murder, calls himself a "fugitive from the ways of this world" and croons a song: "Flyin home / Fly like a motherfucker / Flyin home" (p. 53). Lester's stuffed bear and tiger are washed away in the flooded stream. At the fireworks display at the fair, in a single, affecting scene, he experiences at some level of consciousness pure metaphors of transience and then what seems like an archetypal male dream of women in time.

> High above their upturned faces it burst, sprays of lit glycerine flaring across the night, trailing down the sky in loosely falling ribbons of hot spectra soon burnt to naught. Another went up, a long whishing sound, fishtailing aloft. In the bloom of its opening you could see like its shadow the image of the rocket gone before, the puff of black smoke and ashen trails arcing out and down like a huge and dark medusa squatting in the

sky. In the bloom of light too you could see two men out in the field crouched over their crate of fireworks like assassins or bridgeblowers. And you could see among the faces a young girl with candyapple on her lips and her eyes wide. Her pale hair smelled of soap, womanchild from beyond the years, rapt below the sulphur glow and pitchlight of some medieval fun fair. A lean skylong candle skewered the black pools in her eyes. (p. 65)

Not long before he goes to reclaim his home, he returns to a hillside nearby "to review the country he'd once inhabited." He watches in the distance a wagon that stops at a ford for the mule to drink and then moves on out of sight, its rumbling sound seemingly separated from its motion.

He watched the diminutive progress of all things in the valley, the gray fields coming up black and corded under the plow, the slow green occlusion that the trees were spreading. Squatting there he let his head drop between his knees and he began to cry. (p. 170)

This is homesickness, no doubt, but also deeper homesickness related to the sadness of flux. The cruel language that depicts the processes of seasonal renewal—and of human cultivation of those processes—gives us Lester's distorted view. His grief acknowledges that time is natural and therefore represents all that he himself cannot be. That night, lying awake in his cave, Lester thinks he hears his father whistling on the road, coming home, but then all that he really hears is the running of the stream "through the cavern to empty it may be in unknown seas at the center of the earth" (p. 170).

If Lester were a more sophisticated and reflective person, he would know that what he has experienced, exiled from the security of the normal, is dread. Instead, he has this dream:

He dreamt that night that he rode through woods on a low ridge. Below him he could see deer in a meadow where the sun fell on the grass. The grass was still wet and the deer stood in it to their elbows. He could feel the spine of the mule rolling under him and he gripped the mule's barrel with his legs. Each leaf that brushed his face deepened his sadness and dread. Each leaf he passed he'd never pass again. They rode over his face like veils, already some yellow, their veins like slender bones where the sun shone through them. He had resolved himself to ride on for he could not turn back and the world that day was as lovely as any day that ever was and he was riding to his death. (pp. 170–71)

On one earlier occasion the essence of this vision, and of all such visions, has come to Lester in a less lyrical and more characteristic form. He has brought the hydrocephalic and idiot child of the girl he is making excuses to see a half-frozen robin he has caught. The child chews off the bird's legs, and Lester offers the one explanation that would occur to him: "He wanted it to where it couldn't run off" (p. 79). The connection between this episode and Lester's necrophilia is plain enough, but the necrophilia itself has a prior source in Lester's unprotected exposure to raw time and his conditioned belief that what is living—his mother, his father, and his home—is what is lost. In this novel, since both Lester and the barely human idiot child share that perception, it is represented as being primal.

Lester's continuity with the world is no more complete than his continuity with the community. His whole state of being is one of loss from the beginning, of isolation from the ecological coherence of his environment, both human and unhuman. He is the negative image of Arthur Ownby in *The Orchard Keeper* in this respect, not at home or at ease anywhere. His remote self-containment has somehow metastasized to make him a monster of solipsism and a victim finally of a pathological discontinuity with the world. He is not a resourceful woodsman simply because he is not an observer. He is innocent of, and uninterested in, the nature of the materials of the world and of how processes and procedures produce specific results (and he therefore has no trade). He is oblivious to beauty, either simple or complex, and would as soon shoot a bluebird as not, and for no reason in any case (p. 25); he is unable to notice the transformation of his woods by frozen rain, "grass webbed with little panes of ice . . . the woods garlanded with frostflowers, weeds springing up from white crystal fantasies like the stone lace in a cave's floor" (p. 158).

His relations with other people are marked at various extremes by a reckless willfulness that not only shows his indifference to any structure of human reality other than his own but causes even his courage, his one virtue, to become suspect, since it owes so much to his ignorance of real danger. Hence, for example, his naïve conviction in the beginning that he can stop the auction sale of his land with crude threats and a single-shot .22 rifle.

For Lester there is no check upon the self, no sense of where he leaves off and the other begins—of the difference, in short, between the self and what sets limits to it. What is crazy about him fundamentally is his disconnection from the real, a condition of which the murders and sexual crimes he commits are only lurid symptoms. Whether his inherent dissociation from nature, in the broadest sense, causes him to fear and distrust it or whether his fear and distrust cause him to dissociate himself from it—to neutralize it by internalizing it—the effect is the same; and real people are included in the consequences.

When he is lonely, he simply kills some people to keep him company, to exchange a grotesque parody of love with; yet underlying all of Lester's mad cruelty is the simple fact of human loneliness—in its form as the need for human companionship ("He poured into that waxen ear everything he'd ever thought of saying to a woman" [p. 88]) and in its form as an ungratifiable need to feel at home in the strange world and in the unaccommodating vastness of space.

> False spring came again with a warm wind. The snow melted off into little patches of gray ice among the wet leaves. With the advent of this weather bats began to stir from somewhere deep in the cave. Ballard lying on his pallet by the fire one evening saw them come from the dark of the tunnel and ascend through the hole overhead fluttering wildly in the ash and smoke like souls rising from hades. When they were gone he watched the hordes of cold stars sprawled across the smokehole and wondered what stuff they were made of, or himself. (p. 141)

In order for McCarthy to commend Lester Ballard to our attention and sympathy, it is necessary that he present Lester's story primarily from Lester's own point of view and that he show that his needs and behavior have at least vague affinities with our own. But paradoxically Lester must also remain unanalyzed in order to retain his aspect of mystery, to seem driven finally not by wholly explicable motives but by unknowable cthonic powers; otherwise it becomes too easy to file him away—to incarcerate him, so to speak—in the ordered categories of thought. Lester is worth our attention, presented in this form, because he and his behavior cause us to meditate upon the peculiar, dangerous poetry of violence, like that of the boar that Lester watches under attack by hounds: "Ballard watched this ballet tilt and swirl and churn mud up through the snow and watched the lovely blood welter there in its holograph of battle, spray burst from a ruptured lung, the dark heart's blood, pinwheel and pirouette, until shots rang and all was done" (p. 69). Distance, of whatever kind, enables us to move across a fluid boundary, from reality into story or dream, where anything is then possible because only attitude and what is possible count.

The eerie dream of the world—of which Lester, at one level, is the source of but, at another, is only an aspect—prevails from the beginning of *Child of God* to the end; and it is saved from naïve decadence by an equally constant impingement of the familiar and real—from the wonderfully true dialogue, from the solidity of McCarthy's humorous and stoical country people, and from the steady rhythm of normal life that is the counterpoint of Lester's. But we are jolted permanently out of the range of Lester's enchantment by his last murder, which is both vivid and heartbreaking—and saved for the last, we suspect, because it abruptly reinstates moral sense. As in the previous cases, Lester has surprised a boy and girl parked on a deserted road. He shoots the boy almost immediately when the boy tries to start his truck. Then he says to the terrified girl ("holding her hands in the air as if she didn't know where to put them"):

> You better get out of there.
> What?
> Out. Come on out of there.
> What are you goin to do?
> That's for me to know and you to find out.
> The girl pushed the boy from her and slid across the seat and stepped out into the mud of the road.
> Turn around, Ballard said.
> What are you goin to do?
> Just turn around and never mind.
> I have to go to the bathroom, the girl said.
> You don't need to worry about that, said Ballard.
> Turning her by the shoulder he laid the muzzle of the rifle at the base of her skull and fired.
> She dropped as if the bones in her body had been liquefied. Ballard tried to catch her but she slumped into the mud. He got hold of her dress by the nape to raise her but the material parted in his fist and in the end he had to stand the rifle against the fender of the truck and take her under the arms.
> He dragged her through the weeds, walking backwards, watching over his shoulder. Her head was lolling and blood ran down her neck and Ballard had dragged her out of her shoes. He was breathing harshly and his eyeballs were wild and white. He laid her down in the woods not fifty feet from the road and threw himself on her, kissing the still warm mouth and feeling under her clothes. Suddenly he stopped and raised up. He lifted her skirt and looked down at her. She had wet herself. He cursed and pulled down the panties and dabbed at the pale thighs with the hem of the girl's skirt. (pp. 150–51)

Lester's cruelty is no longer mediated by the pathos of his situation or the exoticism of his crimes, for the context has been humanized by the victim and by the normalness underlying the dialogue between them. As it happens this time, the boy is not dead but revives to drive the truck away. Lester pursues him frantically, to no avail. When he finally makes his way the three miles back up the mountain, the girl is lying as he has left her, legs spread, but "cold and wooden with death"; and when he hauls her out on his shoulders, she rides "with legs bowed akimbo like a monstrous frog" (p. 153). Lester's crimes are a desecration of the human. He has become, like the night riders of *Outer Dark*, an ally and agent of death, transforming the human into ugly matter.

In the structure of existence in *Child of God*, the center, which is the normal, holds firm against its fears of encompassing death, the deformation that turns us into corrupting meat and eventually nothing at all and can do so as instantaneously as the girl Lester kills drops "as if the bones in her body had been liquefied." Center and circumference intersect at the novel's end, when the "high sheriff of Sevier County" and his deputies cross "the field from Willie Gibson's old rifle shop" carrying "muslin shrouds on which was stenciled Property of the State of Tennessee" and find the bodies, dripping rheum, covered with the "gray cheesy mold" of adipocere, and with scallops of fungus growing on them "as they do on logs rotting in the forest" (p. 196). Lester has been the bridge between these two points all along, at home in neither world but indentured to both. He is therefore both responsible, as he knows, and a victim; and in the end he becomes the last vivid instance of the merging with otherness, of the extinction of the inner life.

> His body was shipped to the state medical school at Memphis. There in a basement room he was preserved with formalin and wheeled forth to take his place with other deceased persons newly arrived. He was laid out on a slab and flayed, eviscerated, dissected. His head was sawed open and the brains removed. His muscles were stripped from his bones. His heart was taken out. His entrails were hauled forth and delineated and the four young students who bent over him like those haruspices of old perhaps saw monsters worse to come in their configurations. At the end of three months when the class was closed Ballard was scraped from the table into a plastic bag and taken with others of his kind to a cemetery outside the city and there interred. A minister from the school read a simple service. (p. 194)

We are most aware of Lester's humanness at the point at which it is irrevocably extinguished, and through that paradox McCarthy causes the status of humanness itself to seem intolerably ambiguous and frail—nugatory, even, in the unimplicated, insentient otherness of the world. This in fact is the point that the novel seems to stick on, at the end, out at the edge.

> In the evening a jeep descended the log road towing a trailer in the bed of which lay seven bodies bound in muslin like enormous hams. As they went down the valley in the new fell dark basking nighthawks rose from the dust in the road before them with wild wings and eyes red as jewels in the headlights. (pp. 196–97)

In certain rural areas of the South, the phrase *child of God* refers to children who are mysteriously "not right in the head." McCarthy adapts that usage and gives it grim metaphorical resonance that calls into question not only the nature of the child but, of course, the nature of God himself and his bizarre universe as well. There is the slightest hint in those hawks at the end that it is Lester who is at home and we, the normal ones, who are estranged. Throughout the novel McCarthy has sustained for us the odd illusion that Lester is somehow mysteriously forgiven. This is at once strange and not strange, for if Lester is in a state of grace—if such grace were in fact possible—this seems to be precisely and incomprehensibly what true grace would be like.

IV Death and Affirmation
Suttree

*S*uttree is a novel about transcending death—not in fact, of course, but in the mind and spirit. Death is animate and pervasive in Cornelius Suttree's field of vision, an apotheosis for him of the true world-in-itself—apart from but subjugating the human. It commands all dimensions of human life, consuming bodies and souls and, along with them, what there is of achievement, meaning, and value. This, at any rate, is the way Suttree sees it, the way McCarthy makes it seem.

> The night is quiet. Like a camp before battle. The city beset by a thing unknown and will it come from forest or sea? The murengers have walled the pale, the gates are shut, but lo the thing's inside and can you guess his shape? Where he's kept or what's the counter of his face? Is he a weaver, bloody shuttle shot through a timewarp, a carder of souls from the world's nap? Or a hunter with hounds or do bone horses draw his deadcart through the streets and does he call his trade to each? Dear friend he is not to be dwelt upon for it is by just suchwise that he's invited in. (pp. 4–5)

The thing—death conceived—is inside in one metaphorical form or the other, comforting psychological defenses notwithstanding, and with Suttree it has breached even the walls of consciousness, infecting his will to be. Death in his world diminishes each particular being to pointless corrupting matter, and in the mind it is therefore the objective correlative of a morbid nihilism.

For Suttree this conception is worse than the usual intermittent and normal dread, for he, like Stephen Dedaelus, is an imperfectly lapsed Catholic, left impaled upon the wrong end of a coherent theological dogma in which the world can be only a place of death and suffering and, at best, a dangerous obstacle to salvation. Suttree's world, like that of Dedaelus, brooding cynically on Sandymount Strand, is wholly demystified and only mocked by intimations of grace; yet it bears the indelible, gothic attributes of militant religious instruction, the imprimatur of "Christian witchcraft," as Suttree calls it. Suttree's challenge in the novel is to come to terms with what is; having invited the "thing" in by dwelling upon it, he must either give in to it and die in stages or live and, in living, affirm life. His progression along the better of these two courses is by no means ineluctable or conducted in defined stages, but it does occur, in a restrained, ambiguous, barely perceptible development.

Cornelius Suttree is more sophisticated and reflective than McCarthy's other characters, and he lives in the city rather than the country; but the world that he must make his way in is ultimately the same as theirs, and he achieves his marginal transcendence of it only to the degree that he possesses a more effective array of human resources than they do. These resources, by virtue of being specifically human, are understood also, in the end, to be sacred. The insensate "thing" of this prologue is there within the walls, but so is the sentient human opposing it.

One powerful image near the conclusion of the novel consolidates the many implications that have accrued in this eccentric life-or-death contest. Suttree is on the verge of being reinstated in his life. He goes to find his friend Ab Jones, an older black man, who has made it his life's mission to wage a senseless, heroic war against the police. Suttree fears that Ab has been killed in one last appalling melee; his fears are confirmed when he finds Ab's grieving wife, Doll, at their shanty on the river, which has doubled as a speakeasy and an ad hoc hostel for the down-and-out. Throughout the novel Doll has been mutely stoical, vaguely oracular, primeval even. She has only one good eye; the other has atrophied in its socket.

> How is he? said Suttree. Is he here?
> She shook her head.
> Is he not out of the hospital?
> Yes. He's out. The Lord taken him out. She began to cry, standing there in her housecoat and slippers, holding her shoulders. The tears that ran on her pitted cheek looked like ink. She had her eye closed but the lid that covered the naked socket did not work so well anymore and it sagged in the cavity and struggled up and that raw hole seemed to watch him with some ghastly equanimity, an eye for another kind of seeing like the pineal eye in atavistic reptiles watching through time, through conjugations of space and matter to that still center where the living and the dead are one.
> (p. 447)

DEATH AND AFFIRMATION 71

The pineal organ of some reptiles does in fact have the essential structure of an eye, a third eye; and associated with the brain, it is therefore adapted here to represent a ghastly primal knowledge that, evolutionary advance notwithstanding, is also human—the thing itself within, not as an idea but as a concealed fact of being. The waiting reality of such a subhuman state has been the unifying theme of Suttree's metaphysical nightmares.

> And he saw an idiot in a yard in a leather harness chained to a clothesline and it leaned and swayed drooling and looked out upon the alley with eyes that fed the most rudimentary brain and yet seemed possessed of news in the universe denied right forms, like perhaps the eyes of squid whose simian depths seem to harbor some horrible intelligence. All down past the hedges a gibbering and howling in a hoarse frog's voice, word perhaps of things known raw, unshaped by the constructions of a mind obsessed with form. (p. 427)

This sinister reptilian state is the equivalent of the state of death: a true, unthinkable other, and as much us—though biding its time—as our human grief and achieved forms. Doll's eyes show both contending states—the one shedding tears, the other a naked socket, a raw hole watching with a reptilian, unimplicated composure. This reptilian eye is not just superstition or a metaphor for McCarthy or for Suttree. It is real, and it brings forward into the comparatively new world of human consciousness ancient, unacceptable news. Its authority gives legitimacy and credibility to the garbled language of dreams and visions, disaccommodating abstraction and theory. Its reality is only barely accessible to empirical intellect and is opposed to intellect even at that, but McCarthy makes it make its own sense.

> The turtlemonger held forth his sack. Fine turkles, fat turkles. Turkles for the stew.
> The dreamer would pass but he has let fall the long dark lilac iron of his riflebarrel to bar the way. An outlaw tollsman reeking of woodsmoke and swamp rot and seeking some chiminage dearer than a path so dark could warrant. Or any path at all.
> These be special turkles. Dont pass on without you've give em your consideration.
> To this the traveler did consent. The vendor's face grew crafty. The wet sack collapsing aclatter on the ground. He turns back the mouth.
> Those are not turtles. Oh God they're not turtles. (p. 455)

This nightmare comes upon a delirious Suttree in a hospital where he is on the verge of dying. In its parable form it sets forth an unsettling truth. Turtles after all are only turtles—these are mud turtles and snappers from the polluted river—and one of the reassuring functions of rational intelligence is to keep us in touch with such empirical facts and free us from needless dread. But rational intelligence is not the only means of knowing in this text, and being "freed" by rationality in *Suttree* is dangerously smug and naïve. Hence one not in a dream might look into a sack full of dead turtles and know perfectly well what they are in fact but shudder also with the sudden thought—pressed forward as it were from the pineal eye—that they are something else also, loathsome and beyond knowing, akin to what we are but certainly apart from what we wish to be. One would then have been thrust momentarily into a new zone of understanding of the human position in time and the world, released, like it or not, from the secure shelter of language and exposed to "turkles" where otherwise mere turtles might be.

Like Joyce, McCarthy is acutely conscious at each new turn of phrase or shift in idiom of how language intensifies and heightens, defines and sharpens, or spreads out and projects our reality through layers of time. Notice even here, for instance, the odd and disturbing conjunction—in an otherwise precisely observed descriptive phrase—of "lilac" and "riflebarrel." The connotations are so incompatible that we feel removed for an instant, as if into a surrealist painting. Cornelius Suttree is McCarthy's first informed witness and resisting victim of his fear and knowledge.

Suttree is in fact a new character in McCarthy's work because he brings a new order of experience to McCarthy's now more complex but still recognizable fictional world. To follow the dark path, he has looked into the mouth of the sack upon the "turkles." He is mature, educated, and literate. He has, however, declined to serve the idols of the middle class or even to remain in the world his successful father would choose for him. He has abdicated partly because of the despised example of his father's snobbish tyranny and partly because he wishes to know what his life is fundamentally and whether in the midst of death there can be life to be affirmed. Having invited in the thing, the destroyer, he is no longer able to evade such truth by absolutizing conventional goals. He prefers to live authentically, even in suffering and deprivation, rather than to live in falsehood in comfort. For him alone among his derelict friends this choice is a real one.

DEATH AND AFFIRMATION 73

Suttree lives by fishing in the city's river, setting trotlines for catfish and carp, which he sells to neighborhood fishmarkets—or, as frequently, gives away. This passive occupation, entailing only a minimal commitment of ingenuity and resource, eventually takes on metaphorical suggestions. It draws together other indications that Suttree is putting life to a test, requiring, or allowing, it to prove its worth on its own terms. His lack of volition is a form of receptiveness, and it corresponds to his indifference to sustained philosophical discourse, either with others or with himself. We perceive that he—unlike *Suttree*'s other characters—is capable of understanding and of subscribing to any one of a number of the theories of existence that serve to get one through it, but he eschews theory as vehemently as he does middle-class industry and sobriety. He observes experience obsessively but only as raw fact, and he construes it only in the eidetic language of heightened images and dreams. Like McCarthy's earlier work, *Suttree* is a novel in which theme is not in the foreground, but in this case it is not because the protagonist himself suppresses it. He detranscends, so to speak, in order to discover a meaningful form of transcendence; he surrenders himself to the instructive power of negative capability.

Suttree's river—the Tennessee River, though never named—is no clear-running mountain stream but a polluted, torpid reincarnation of the swamp that Ernest Hemingway's Nick Adams called tragic and was afraid to wade into, an oppressive lowest common denominator of being in Suttree's world.

> Bearing along garbage and rafted trash, bottles of suncured glass wherein corollas of mauve and gold lie exploded, orangepeels ambered with age. A dead sow pink and bloated and jars and crates and shapes of wood washed into rigid homologues of viscera and empty oilcans locked in eyes of dishing slime where the spectra wink guiltily. One day a dead baby. Bloated, pulpy rotted eyes in a bulbous skull and little rags of flesh trailing in the water like tissuepaper. Oaring his way lightly through the rain among these curiosa he felt little more than yet another artifact leached out of the earth and washed along, draining down out of the city, that cold and grainy shape beyond the rain that no rain could make clean again. (p. 306)

This symbolic river flows like an unacknowledged source of being, carrying its refuse with it "through peaceful farmland, high fields tilted on the slopes and rich turned earth in patches of black corrugation among the greening purlieus and small cultivated orchards like scenes of plenitude from picturebooks suddenly pasted over the waste he was a familiar of." It wells "heavy and septic past [the] fine homes on the north shore" (p. 119). A demented evangelist shouts down at Suttree from the isolation of his decaying house: "Back for the fishing are ye? God himself don't look too close on what lies on that river bottom" (p. 412). But Suttree lives there by choice, for the time being, on a subsiding houseboat, a precarious catwalk connecting him to the shore. The river as a symbol incorporates the adversary world around it, drawing all vanity, meaning, and illusion into it, as a black hole is said to consume light.

The river's function for the novel is pointedly overdetermined—it embodies that which calls everything into question—but it is also a metaphorical condensation of the authority of the physical world in *Suttree* generally; and the sheer presence, in weight and mass, of the physical world of *Suttree* is in itself a powerful thematic pressure. We experience the substance of the world not only more vividly than we do in most novels but more vividly than we do in our daily lives. Detail is etched and dense and yet proliferates far past the requirements of conventional realism. The effect of this care is gratifying and entrancing, for though the world is radically desacralized in the process, it is somehow also magically present to us, so that what the dark river will corrupt and carry away is always already being restored—as even in the passage just cited "corollas of mauve and gold lie exploded" in bottles of "suncured glass."

> The boy was ladling a great load of beans aboard his plate. Suttree buttered one of the buoyant looking soda biscuits and watched the pale slices of pork fall under the knife, the man turning the roast and finally seizing it in his hands, the white knob of bone coming from its socket with a sucking sound and breaking like a great pearl up through the steaming meat. (p. 313)

> In the morning he went down early and as he passed the houseboat he saw a young girl come out along the little veranda and turn and squat, her skirts gathered in the crooks of her elbows. Through the fog Suttree was presented with a bony pointed rump. She pissed loudly into the river and rose and went in again. (p. 307)

> The river was frozen between the houseboat and the bank, a thin skim of wrinkled ice through which fell chunks of frozen mud from the underside of the flexing plank. He threw the empty basket up on the wagon and took the full one from the old man. (p. 163)

He [Gene Harrogate] rose and started down the hill toward the road and toward the creekside jungle where the pigs had gone. As he went he studied the pens scattered among the trees on the hillside above him, eclectic shelters hammered up out of snuff signs and boards and odds of fencing all hung in plumbless suspension down the bald and raingutted slope. He could see no one hunting hogs. When he struck the path along the creek he could see the tracks of the pigs here and there in the patches of black mire like the delicately pointed prints of small deer. Coming past a collection of old waterheaters he started them and they flushed into the wall of ivy with high raspy snorts. He picked one out and dove after it. It went through a mass of vines and over a mound of broken fruitjars and disappeared with an agonizing squall. Harrogate fetched up in a small clearing. He had tilted himself into a locust tree and was bleeding in several places. He could hear the pigs diminishing in the distance.

When they came out on the riverbank at the point they paused to test the air. They started downstream at about the time that Harrogate emerged from the brush and they checked and swung back along the creek, their noses dishing and their eyes white. They defiled down a gully to the water and bunched and jerked their noses at it and came back. Harrogate was closing on them like a gangly tiptoe spider. They veered with new alarm and snuffled and went on down the point.

Looky here at these pigs daddy.

A man rose up from the tall grass where he'd been sitting and put his hand on top of his hat and turned around. The pigs flared like quail. They passed Harrogate some to the left and some to the right all screaming and he looked about and threw himself finally in the general direction of the pigs and landed full length with a grunt.

When he came upon them next they were feeding in a bower of honeysuckle, turning up the black earth and devouring worms and grubs and roots with subdued hoggish joy. (p. 138)

In the third week of August it began to rain. He and the boy were on the river when it started and the rain was very cold and they tucked their necks against it and put toward shore. Not drops but whole glycerinous clots of water were falling in the river, raising great bladderlike weals that exchanged with constant hissing pops. The boy's hat came slowly and darkly down about his face like a flower in an inkbottle until he looked out from a soggy cowl, his back hunched and his eyes planing about in deep suspicion. Suttree at the oars grinned. The boy half grinned back. His whole head was turning pale blue with hatdye. (p. 356)

Below the bridge, he eased himself erect, took up the oars and began to row toward the south bank. There he brought the skiff about, swinging the stern into a clump of willows, and going aft he raised up a heavy cord that ran into the water from an iron pipe driven into the mud of the bank. This he relayed through an open oarlock mounted on the skiff's transom. Now he set out again, rowing slowly, the cord coming up wet and smooth through the lock and dipping into the river again. When he was some thirty feet from shore the first dropper came up, doubling the line until he reached and cast it off. He went on, the skiff lightly quartered against the river's drift, the hooks riding up one by one into the oarlock with their leached and tattered gobbets of flesh. When he felt the weight of the first fish he shipped the dripping oars and took hold of the line and brought it in by hand. A large carp broke water, a coarse mailed flank dull bronze and glinting. He braced himself with one knee and hefted it into the boat and cut the line and tied on a fresh hook with a chunk of cutbait and dropped it over the side and went on, sculling with one oar, the carp warping heavily against the floorboards.

When he had finished running the line he was on the other side of the river. He rebaited the last drop and let the heavy cord go, watching it sink in the muddy water among a spangled nimbus of sunmotes, a broken corona up through which flared for a moment the last pale chunk of rancid meat. (pp. 7-8)

Since the people who inhabit this environment of *Suttree* are correspondingly solid and express their natures seemingly in relation to it alone, free of thematic role, character and setting are meaningfully coextensive. The Dickenslike fictional characters seem to run their own show in a space that is persuasively three-dimensional, dense with odors and flavors and sounds and configurations of action and movement—that is, wholly untheoretical—the squalid and beautiful alternating and intersecting unpredictably and convincingly. Entering a world so manifest and substantial, so unresponsive to metaphysics, and yet so complex and mystifying and unstable, one can understand the need to reckon with it on its own terms and perhaps conclude, as Suttree will, that on those terms it is sufficient unto itself.

> Through the thin and riven wall sounds of fish surging in the sinking skiff. The sign of faith. Twelfth house of the heavens. Ushering in the western church. St Peter patron of fishmongers. St Fiacre that of piles. Suttree placed one arm across his eyes. He said that he might have been a fisher of men in another time but these fish now seemed task enough for him. (p. 14)

This is not about achieving a religious faith that overreaches the world but about reconciliation to the world itself, task enough, as Suttree says, considering the mixed signals it sends forth.

Suttree's elliptical meditations and dreams always exhibit the mixture of sacred and secular idioms shown here, the one adapted to the other. He is a lapsed Catholic and therefore also a kind of a secular hierophant, on watch for even waning evidence of the sacred within the profane. And yet, significantly, even his most bizarre hallucinations are anchored securely in circumstantial reality.

> That evening he passed through a children's cemetery set in a bench of hillside and forlorn save by weeds. The stone footings of a church nearby was all the church there was and leaves fell few and slowly, here and here, him reading the names, the naked headboards all but perished in the weathers of seasons past, these tablets tilted or fallen, titles to small plots of earth against all claiming. A storm had followed him for days. He turned in an ashen twilight, crossing this garden of the early dead by weeds the wind has sown. Brown jasmine among the nettles. He saw small figurines composed of dust and light turn in the broken end of a bottle, spider-sized marionettes in some minute ballet there in the purple glass so lightly strung with strands of cobweb floss. A drop of rain sang on a stone. Bell loud in the wild silence. Harried mute and protestant over the darkening windy fields he saw go with no surprise mauve monks in cobwebbed cowls and sandals hacked from ruined boots clapping along in a rude shuffle down small cobbled ways into an old stone town. Storm birds rode up dark and chattering and burst away like ash and mice were going down their homeward furrows like tailed shot. (pp. 286–87)

In this section Suttree's very sanity is in question, and yet the dense lyrical idiom shows the relation between subject and object to have achieved a strangely grounded stability. Like the syntax, "crossing this garden of the early dead by weeds the wind has sown," the metaphors and similes of the passage hold us poetically at a distance from what is actually being seen—birds like ash, mice like tailed shot—and the detail of the monks' sandals hacked from ruined boots hardly seems observable from the implied perspective. But a world with distinct edges is clearly there behind the layers of stylization, minutely registered even if the descriptive vocabulary holds us suspended in a zone between it and the world of mind and words—even if, in fact, all of what seems to be there is not, like the monks, really there at all. Whatever is happening in *Suttree*, the world in itself is always insisting upon its own reality; it is there to be dealt with as itself and not simply at the subordinated service of ideas. Suttree's own inner life, the very idiom of his thinking, shows that he is attuned to the world as itself and that he bears a reluctant allegiance to it. It is, after all—God being absent from the world—his only recourse.

In this regard it is instructive to compare the texture of *Suttree*, an extension of the naturalistic tradition in American fiction, with the purest example of the romance tradition, *The Great Gatsby*. Aside from all of the obvious differences—of subject, character, setting and theme—a fundamental and instructive difference between two such novels is one of gravitational force. Our sense of the irreality of Gatsby's dreamed world is a function in part of its perceived weight; its relative mass is an extension of Gatsby's illusion of what is possible. It is an unearthly earth, its detail, in turn, almost wholly metaphorical at one level or another. And Fitzgerald is careful to insist upon the dangerous ironies of such dissociation even while he ingeniously fabricates the gossamer, alluring texture of that setting as if he were Gatsby himself. The novel's brilliance, in fact, owes primarily to Fitzgerald's success in sustaining this subtly dualistic perspective—an effect that Carraway is oddly incidental to; and the novel's first genuine shock, as a consequence, is not so much Myrtle Wilson's death as the sheer, inert mass of her body, oddly kneeling in the road, chest torn open, irreparably dead. Myrtle's body, which Gatsby never sees and refuses to hear about, is the unassimilated mass that is absent from this otherwise ghostly mind's world; and it contradicts it. Gatsby had envisioned "that the sidewalks really formed a ladder and mounted to a secret place among the trees" and that "he could climb to it, if he climbed alone, and once there ... could suck on the pap of life, gulp down the incomparable milk of wonder." Cornelius Suttree, starting out in a higher station of life, reverses this process; and the impersonal, unsubjectified authority of the world he reaches is correspondingly unsubmissive and uncooperative. Faith is a real task at this end, for it involves accommodating one's ideas to the world as it is.

McCarthy's usually unselfconscious realism—obedient to the truth of objects—is a theme itself, not simply a medium through which theme is conveyed. The high proportion of raw material, in the larger span of structure and in the smaller span of phrase—as with the girl urinating, holding her skirts not just up but in the crooks of her elbows—is his novel's way of expressing how rich the world is on the one hand, how unhumanized it is on the other, and how irrelevant to anything except our own inner lives our Gatsbylike dreams of it are. Still, though McCarthy in the traditional philosophical sense is not, to say the least, an idealist, he is no more willing than his surrogate, Suttree, to give in to the appalling gravity of utter materialism. A kind of détente is achieved, as, one imagines, the best to be hoped for; and the novel makes its way surreptitiously toward that outcome by developing dialectically a simple tension between human perseverance and unaccommodating fact.

One of the reasons that our sense of the world as an entity is so vivid in *Suttree* is that so much of the action of the novel is given over to arduous feats of sheer physical labor. True, many of these exertions are ludicrously quixotic or baroque and are almost necessarily executed by people who are otherwise not at all intimate with what society calls productive work. But work in *Suttree* is work as itself, calling upon muscle, patience, stamina, aggravation, and sweat and requiring dealing with the stubborn materiality of the world, either maddeningly inert or violently, elusively in motion. The fourth of the extracts in the series recently cited (p. 75), for instance, represents less than a third of a long, harrowing, and hilarious narrative sequence describing Gene Harrogate's pursuit and final capture of a neighbor's loose pig, followed by an excruciatingly detailed account of his efforts to clean and flay it with only a shoplifted pocketknife. (He ends up, of course, merely mutilating it.)

One of Suttree's other loony companions, Leonard, a "part-time catamite" (p. 241), harasses Suttree into helping him bury his dead father in the river so that the welfare agents won't discover that his mother has been drawing social security checks on a decomposing dead man for six months. This procedure involves hauling the decayed and stinking body out of the trunk of a car, dragging it down to the river and trussing it in chains and several stolen wheel rims, and then rowing it downstream to dump it into the black water under the railway bridge—this last after an inconclusive discussion of what words would be appropriate to say over it. Later on, the body floats back up, chains and all, and is discovered ("Fathers will do that," Suttree says [p. 417]); later still, the dead father has to be exhumed and evicted from his perpetual-care grave plot because Leonard's mother has fallen behind on her payments and it is repossessed.

Suttree himself, irrational with anger and grief, fills in his own son's grave with only a spade, working from midafternoon until nightfall, while the gravediggers and cemetery workers look on, mildly bemused, with their tractor and frontloader standing idly by. (A great deal of the labor in *Suttree* is associated somehow with death, as if intended to remind us subliminally of the twin, irreversible consequences of the Fall. Even the ambulance that comes to pick up the corpse in Suttree's houseboat at the end of the novel gets stuck in the mire up to its differential and has to be pushed out by three black boys who pass by.) One of Suttree's companions makes his living flinging himself in front of city buses and then filing injury suits; and though this is not work in the conventional sense, it is certainly arduous and certainly physical and an odd parody of how the poor in Suttree's adopted community resourcefully make do with their fate. The only legitimate job Gene Harrogate holds, briefly, entails dismantling for salvage the seats of a car that has been demolished in a head-on collision with a tractor-trailer rig. The doors are jammed, and Harrogate has to contrive to force them open from the inside. Bits of matter cling to the windshield; burgundy-black blood stains the upholstery. He finds a human eye inside, still attached to its muscle and nerve fibers. (We are reminded by this, in a way that is typical of the novel's subtle subject rhyme, of Doll's eye and what it means.)

Suttree, of course, mainly tends his trotlines, but during one long period he is involved in work that is Sisyphean by comparison. He becomes a partner in a mussel-shell-gathering enterprise conducted upstream by a family named Reese in the shoals of the French Broad River. The men do the brailing, and the women clean the mussels from the shells. The shells are then sold for forty dollars a ton. ("Them little fellas is heavier than what you might think," says Reese to skeptical Suttree [p. 312].) The process is agonizingly slow and even on a successful run involves the steady exertion of rowing a boatload of mussels back upstream to the camp.

> When they drifted out into the slow water at the foot of their run amid flotsam and tranquil spume the boy stood at the transom and hauled the brail aboard and hung it dripping in the uprights with a couple dozen black mussels clamped to the lines. They swung and turned and clacked and the boy took out an enormous brass cookspoon and began to pry them loose. Within minutes they lay like stones in the floor of the skiff and the boy had cast the brail overboard again. He turned to Suttree who was backoaring to stand in the current. His face was flushed and his breath short. That's how we do it, he wheezed.
> Is that a pretty good batch for a run?
> It aint no more'n average. I've seen em to come up solid with em. Me and Daddy has dredged messes we couldn't lift. (p. 324)

At the end of the summer, heavy rains come down to their river camp. Suttree and the family spend three days shoveling mussels at one site away from the edge of the swollen river; when they go downstream to check the other site, they find "part of the bank washed out and a great crescent-shaped bite gone from their stacks" (p. 357). The same rain one night washes a wall of slate loose above the camp, and Reese's daughter, Wanda—Suttree's beguiling lover as well—is killed beneath the landslide. In the harrowing aftermath Reese takes up her crushed body and stumbles, grieving, into the rainy darkness. Otherwise buoyant and full of hope, Reese now falls and kneels in the rain and cries out—"to the darkness over them all"—"Oh God I caint take no more. Please lift this burden from me for I caint bear it" (p. 363). It is a cry not only of grief and loss but of exhaustion as well, a cry against the burden of surviving in the world and against the labor of keeping one's hopes up under the weight of its force.

Reese and a small cluster of Suttree's other friends—Billy Ray Callahan, Ab Jones, Gene Harrogate—considered together form an odd little band of ragtag existential heroes, each defining life in his own exclusive terms and each finding his own symbolic leverage against necessity. Each acts out in some specific way the principle that not having any real choice about things makes it necessary to choose.

Reese is a believer. He never doubts that his mussel-shell operation will pay off for all, even at forty dollars a ton. He never doubts that he can sell his mussel pearls to someone. He never doubts that he can double his money in any tong game. And his exuberance and trust in part do change his luck and alter outcomes. The simple beauty of his generosity and spirit seems to overcome entirely the settings that are forced upon him, as if an odd radiance had transformed the scenes, which are in themselves pathetically austere and squalid. And, of course, in the end the setting reclaims its own preeminence with the death of Wanda, fact finally breaking its way through his aura of optimistic denial. The enthusiasm of both Reese and Harrogate runs across the grain of tragic reality but is all the more powerful in the book because of that. Suttree watches and learns from the two men, perhaps without knowing it; their positive influence affects his intellectual growth and collaborates with other influences that move him off the dead center of his nihilistic immobility.

Billy Ray Callahan and Ab Jones are fighters, placing themselves in conflict with the law as a matter of principle, acting out jeopardy with serious intent and consequences. Callahan's is the simpler case. The man is boyish and good-hearted and a loyal, protective friend; but he loves brawls inside jail and out, and with his belligerent Irish innocence out in front, he either picks them or joins them with gusto, beaming with satisfaction, bloody and happy in his life's work. He is mortally wounded, with his hands uncharacteristically in his pockets, smirking at the tavern bouncer who has just shot him in the face. He lives on for five hours in the hospital emergency room, breathing steadily, as if holding out to prove a point. When he finally lets go, the scene is touchingly, ironically Homeric. "When the doctor came out and told them he was dead Billy Ray's mother began to cry very quietly. She sat there with her chin quivering and she shook her head slowly from side to side over her dead warrior. Suttree touched her shoulder but she waved him away and she did not look up" (p. 377). In some other context, Billy Ray's good-natured bellicosity would seem frivolous—and making an issue of it irresponsible; in this context, because of the abstractness of the forces that bear down on everyone from any side, abstract rebellion seems a worthwhile cause, whatever form it might take.

Ab Jones's case is both similar and different. A massive black man, friend and adviser to Suttree, he runs a beer and gambling joint up the river from Suttree's houseboat. When he is not on duty there, he is out in the streets at night pursuing a crazed vendetta against the Knoxville police. He is scarred, broken, and dented from these wars but keeps his life meaningful by continuing the clearly doomed conflict. "Bein a nigger is an interestin life," he says once to Suttree, home battered and taped-up from jail. "You make it that way," Suttree says, and Ab agrees: "Maybe" (p. 203). But Ab's fatalism is more than merely racial: "You see a man, he scratchin to make it. Think once he got it made everthing be all right. But you dont never have it made. Dont care who you are. Look up one mornin and you a old man. You aint got nothin to say to your brother. Dont know no more'n when you started" (p. 203).

Ab's conflict with the police seems vaguely theological, as if he had displaced his resentment toward an unapparent God onto His tangible and all too willing emissaries on earth. "They dont like no nigger walkin around like a man," he says of them (p. 203), thus bridging an existential gap. On the last night of his freedom, already exhausted beyond all vanity from fighting and being drunk, he goads two fresh, white policemen into battle by telling them gratuitously to fuck themselves. Suttree has been attempting to carry him home from the alley where he has found him, barely conscious. But when these policemen arrive, Ab raises himself to stand erect "with a strength and grace contrived out of absolute nothingness" (p. 440); and then he fights and is eventually killed. It is the emphasis here upon the contrivance of strength that promotes the special illusion of Ab's representative dignity. (Suttree has earlier said over the body of an old ragman who has long since given up in self-pitying despair, "You have no right to represent people in this way. . . . A man is all men" [p. 422].) People in this world are, as Doll's eyes will show, part nothing—identified with matter and death, known only to a reptilian eye-brain—and part human; and the human part is real only to the extent that it is contrived. Ab, more even than the youthful Billy Ray, embodies resistance as a renewing tragic end in itself.

Suttree is a thickly populated novel—Dickensian in this respect—and both the novel's brisk pace and its cheerfully episodic and elliptical progress contribute to the illusion that the people in the book have taken command of its structure. And since these proliferating characters are seen by us at, so to speak, Suttree's eye level and since all seem to have several different familiar names, there often appear to be even more of them than there really are. But for all the novel's rhetorical and generalized preoccupation with evil in the scheme of the world, there is hardly any sense conveyed of a specifically *human* evil—as in Faulkner's *Sanctuary*, say, or even *Light in August* or McCarthy's own two previous novels. The implied attitude toward human nature is remarkably benign—close to being sentimental and unconvincing in the aggregate. Even the forces of oppression—representatives of middle-class shibboleths such as Suttree's father or of gratuitous injustice such as the police—are shadowy to start with and are kept pretty much offstage throughout, as in cartoon strips that exclude full images of adults altogether.

A result of this uncharacteristically Pelagian view of human society is the odd dualism of the novel that requires one to speak vaguely of the world on the one hand and of a separate human position within it on the other. That distinction is not arbitrary either; it is a major philosophical distinction of the book, and Suttree's experience among his indefatigable friends, as they exchange unverbalized messages—embodying truth, Yeats would say, rather than knowing it—becomes the means by which Suttree comes to know what he can of it and to act finally upon its implications. Tragic outcomes are inevitable. The character of the world ensures that. But the novel's prevailing spirit is an oddly happy one, as if adversity itself made the overcoming of it possible and joyful. Nietzsche speaks in the orchestration of these events. So does this anonymous survivor of Belsen (cited by D. J. Enright in *The Oxford Book of Death*): "In my happier days I used to remark on the aptitude of the saying, 'when in life we are in the midst of death.' I have since learnt that it's more apt to say, 'when in death we are in the midst of life.'" Adversity is the common matrix of both tragic and comic transcendence. When the latter prevails, we are, in death, in the midst of life.

This point requires emphasizing and bearing in mind because it helps explain how Suttree's alter ego and coprotagonist, Gene Harrogate, enriches the novel's fatalistic theme as well as its narrative and its outrageous comedy. Like Reese, Harrogate never doubts his capacity to prevail over circumstances or his right to. He is an enterprising survivor for whom the jeopardy of raw poverty is an exhilarating game. When the game comes to an end for him, it is because of the very innocence that sustained it in the first place—in effect because of his inability to consider the difference between the way the world is and the way he imagines it to be, or to gauge accurately the margin between him and it.

Harrogate is exuberantly resourceful because he is an innocent; Suttree is existentially paralyzed because he is not. Practically a boy and known as the country mouse and the city rat and—for good reason—the moonlight melon-mounter, Harrogate is innately oblivious to such immobilizing, bourgeois distractions as ontological insecurity. Innocence and amorality are linked in him, and it is therefore only a matter of time before the world that is not Harrogate expresses itself in the form of law. A rare reflective exchange with Suttree early in the novel foreshadows this outcome.

> Sometimes in the evening Suttree would bring beers and they'd sit there under the viaduct and drink them. Harrogate with questions of city life.
> You ever get so drunk you kissed a nigger?
> Suttree looked at him. Harrogate with one eye narrowed on him to tell the truth. I've been a whole lot drunker than that, he said.
> Worst thing I ever done was to burn down old Lady Arwood's house.
> You burned down an old lady's house?
> Like to of burnt her down in it. I was put up to it. I wasnt but ten year old.
> Not old enough to know what you were doing.
> Yeah.—Hell no that's a lie. I knowed it and done it anyways.
> Did it burn completely down?
> Plumb to the ground. Left the chimbley standin was all. It burnt for a long time fore she come out.

> Did you not know she was in there?
> I disremember. I dont know what I was thinkin. She come out and run to the well and drawed a bucket of water and thowed it at the side of the house and then just walked on off towards the road. I never got such a whippin in my life. The old man like to of killed me.
> Your daddy?
> Yeah. He was alive then. My sister told them deputies when they come out to the house, they come out there to tell her I was in the hospital over them watermelons, she told em I didnt have no daddy was how come I got in trouble. But shit fire I was mean when I did have one. It didnt make no difference.
> Were you sorry about it? The old lady's house I mean.
> Sorry I got caught. (pp. 144–45)

In the right context, or given a damaging knock on the head, Harrogate could as easily be a Lester Ballard simply because of the ease with which he transcends normal restraints. Even his otherwise comical infatuation with watermelons—an extreme version of his making do off what comes to hand—is clouded for us slightly by the memory of Lester and his bizarre innocence. But Harrogate is sane in a way that Lester is not, and Harrogate knows and innocently takes responsibility for what he is. ("It occurred to [Suttree] that other than the melon caper he'd never heard the city rat tell anything but naked truth" [p. 145].) For the novel's larger concerns it is the full curve of Harrogate's experience that matters, not just the uninhibited high comedy Harrogate provides. He starts out in a bumpkin's Eden of consciousness and remains there for longer than one would think possible and then ends up headed for Brushy Mountain Prison, lost to himself in the world. The one end of the experience is as important as the other, since Harrogate's story is preeminently a celebration of ingenuity, an episodic parody of imagination striking back against reality.

Harrogate is able to survive as well as he does and for as long as he does because he thrives on challenge and because, like Reese, he projects upon any circumstance the most cheerful possible interpretation. As with Reese, we are screened from the ugly reality of his circumstances by the aura of his perception of them. He makes his home beneath a city viaduct that "spans a jungly gut filled with rubble and wreckage and a few packing-crate shacks inhabited by transient blacks" down through which "puling waste" run the "dark and leprous waters of a creek" threading sumac and poison ivy, leaving a highwater mark of "oil and sewage and condoms dangling in the branches like stranded leeches" (p. 116). Inside—between the arches where the viaduct runs to earth—when Harrogate first enters, there are bones, broken glass, stray dog turds, and two "bent and mangled parking meters with clots of concrete about their roots." Harrogate is stunned by his good fortune at finding it: "Boy," he says. "It'd really be slick if it wasnt took, wouldnt it? I mean being uptown like it is and all." And after having settled in with amenities he has foraged in the night—tin cans to cook in, a mattress stolen from a porch, warning lanterns stolen from construction sites—he invites Suttree to share with him his stew made of pigeons he has caught in a grain-baited rattrap. "Livin uptown like this," he says, "you can find pret near anything you need" (p. 118).

We are hardly ever able to think clearly about Harrogate's dismal situations for thinking about Harrogate *in* his dismal situations, so vividly does he transcend them. He cannot swim but paddles about in the river happily in a boat he has made by welding together matched hoods from two junkyard Fords, trusting some unpublicized principle of buoyancy in existence to keep him safe. He is oblivious to his own appearance, "not loveable," it is said, "adenoidal leptosome" crouching like a "wizened bird, his razorous shoulderblades jutting in the thin cloth of his striped shirt" (p. 54). Sly and rat-faced, Suttree thinks.

When Harrogate is turned out of the workhouse and tracks Suttree down, he is wearing for a shirt "an enormous pair of striped drawers," his neck sticking "through the ripped seam of the crotch, his arms hanging from the capacious legholes like sticks" (p. 114). What he chooses to remember from his year in the workhouse is not the deprivation or indignity or boredom but racing lizards in the kitchen with "old crazy Bodine."

> We'd get the yard man to get em for us. We'd race em on the kitchen floor. Get a bet up. Shit. I had me one named Legs Diamond that son of a bitch would stand straight up with them old legs just a churnin and quick as he'd get traction he was gone like a striped assed ape. Never would touch down with his front feet.
>
> The city mouse shook his head, deep in the fondness of these recollections like a strange little old man there in the blue winter twilight under the bridge. Remembering the sunlight on the buffed floor and the broomhandles laid out and the chalk marks. Lying like the children they were on the cool floor with their fragile reptiles, the small hearts hammering in the palms of their hands. Holding them by their tiny pumping waists and

releasing them at a signal. The lizards rearing onto their hind legs as their feet slipped on the smooth waxed concrete, strange little saurians. (p. 437)

For reading matter Harrogate has a stash of stolen horror comics, "risible picturetales of walking green cadavers and drooling ghouls" (p. 144). Uninnocent Suttree's *dreams* are this way and not at all risible. A mutual acquaintance—a drunken, aggravated junkman—once says to Harrogate impatiently, his tolerance for eccentricity easily exhausted: "How do you sons of bitches find me?" and Harrogate responds, saying the truth as usual, "It aint but just me" (p. 209).

Harrogate's transcendence of circumstance takes the form usually of baroque schemes for making money extralegally. When he learns that the health department is paying a bounty on dead bats (because of a rabies scare), he contrives to collect a whole croker sack full by firing poisoned meat into the twilight air with a slingshot. When his scheme is detected at the hospital, the mystified physician on duty offers him a dollar and a quarter to persuade him to reveal how he had done it. After hearing the story, the doctor says, "Well, I'm sorry your efforts were for nothing." "Maybe a dollar and a quarter aint nothin to you," Harrogate says, "but it is to me" (p. 219). Another scheme entails blowing through the wall of what he takes to be the bank vault, exposed in a vast cave underneath the city. When it turns out that it is the sewer main instead, he is buried beneath the city's refuse. Suttree finds him there after a search, and he is already bouncing back. "I hate for anybody to see me like this," he says, and then: "I'd give ten dollars for a glass of ice water ... Cash money" (p. 277). Suttree, a compulsive reader of signs, looks at Harrogate in his shreds of clothing, covered in dried sewage, and thinks, "True views of man here below" (p. 276). Suttree has turned his flashlight away from Harrogate's face; Harrogate is staring down into the pool of light it makes, already, as it were, seeing his way out.

The caves that Harrogate strives to exploit and is very nearly lost in have emitted, from the time Harrogate discovers them, clear, if faint, symbolic signals—for us, attuned by our proximity to Suttree, but not for Harrogate, who is free of the tyranny of signification. So we are prepared to read Harrogate's relation to the caves and his experience in them as matters of thematic consequence, to read the caves as that which calls identity into question. Even Harrogate himself seems to have a brief foreboding epiphany, as we will see, though he manages predictably to shake it off. The caves extend in all directions beneath the oblivious city, their dangerous hollowness threatening the naïve stability of the world of men above. ("What if a whole goddamned building were to just up and sink? What about two or three buildings? What about a whole block? Harrogate was waving his bottle about. Goddamn, he said. What if the whole fuckin city was to cave in? That's the spirit, said Suttree" [p. 259].) As Harrogate works with his maps with diminishing confidence, there appears to him to be no chartable relationship, real or symbolic, "between the above and the below" (p. 262), as if above and below existed in two entirely separate dimensions. Everywhere Harrogate goes in the caves, a "liquid dripping" follows him, "something gone awry in the earth's organs to which this measured bleeding clocked a constantly eluded doom" (p. 261).

When Suttree searches for Harrogate, he goes past progressively older names and dates carved into the cave wall until he is past human sign altogether, in no time, where only strange mineral shapes and primitive life forms prevail. It is in this setting that Harrogate is exposed for the first time—and not the last—to an unimaginable fact about identity.

> He left [the candle] burning there and went as far as the edge of the light, his small shadow swallowed up finally in the greater dark beyond. He turned and came back. He squatted and watched the flame totter. The dank stone room grew smaller, drew in about him. He crouched in the smallest cup of light with his hands joined at the back of the flame as if he would gather it to him. Hot oil ran on the stones. The wick toppled and dropped with a thin hiss and dark closed over him so absolute that he became without boundary to himself, as large as all the universe and small as anything that was. (pp. 274–75)

Suttree has tried to warn Harrogate about solipsism before, though of course not in so many words. The first winter that Harrogate spends in Knoxville is savagely cold, and he is unable to keep himself warm in his austere quarters. He tells Suttree that he believes it must be the end of the world. Suttree says:

> What?
> Harrogate was looking at the pavement. He said it again.
> Look at me, Suttree said.
> He looked up. Sad pinched face, streaked with grime.
> Are you serious?
> Well what do you think about it?
> Suttree laughed.

DEATH AND AFFIRMATION   89

It aint funny, said Harrogate.
You're funny, you squirrely son of a bitch. Do you think the world will end just because you're cold?
It aint just me. It's cold all over.
It's not cold by Rufus's stove. Now get your ass up there. I'll see you later. (p. 173)

When Harrogate is arrested finally and is sent to the state penitentiary, he is made by McCarthy, in a passage of remarkable power and insight, to seem virtually to disappear. On the train to Brushy Mountain Prison, Harrogate is without thoughts; he merely watches from his window, seeing things as they pass: a cornfield and the dark earth between dead stalks, flocks of nameless birds, winter trees against a winter sky, a woman tossing a dishpan of water into the yard and wiping her hands on her apron, a little store at a crossing, a row of lighted henhouses, a lighted midnight cafe. Then, abruptly, as the train moves into the dark, rainy country, the windows become tear-stained black mirrors: "and the city rat could see his pinched face watching him back from the cold glass, out there racing among the wires and the bitter trees, and he closed his eyes" (p. 439).

To think of Harrogate dispersed into the world and then to remember him free, contriving his endless baroque schemes, is to perceive the real and metaphorical horror of prison life, of passivity and inaction, and to consider how it is that schemes and scheming hold the world at bay. This long, saddening account of Harrogate's journey has begun with the observation—his or the narrator's—"It is true the world is wide." The dreadful reality within the cliché—that we are not the world nor the world us—would not be likely to occur to Harrogate as a thought, but it has entered his mind; and we experience it his way. A childish solipsism has been Harrogate's redemption from the beginning, so it is appropriate that his defeat takes the form of, or coincides with, its dispersal. When he is finally arrested, he has been caught breaking into a store. It seems unlike Harrogate, too crude and unelaborate. His breaking into a store in fact seems like a gesture of defeat, as if, unprepared for it, he had suddenly grown up and is therefore in some sense, before he heads off to prison, gone already.

When Harrogate has that perception of the self's arbitrariness in the context of the not-self, he is telepathically in communication with Suttree, for whom ontological anxiety is a recurring crisis. Both characters in different ways bring into focus the contest of the self and the world. Suttree has such an experience himself, but for him it comes as an act of volition, a surrender to self-annihilation. In October he takes in his trotlines and hikes into the mountains, ostensibly to escape the persistent reappearances of an ancient geechee witch and the terrors of death she releases. The adventure starts out as a rite of purification for him and ends, after weeks of starvation and solitude, on the border of madness. The first stage of this outcome begins when "everything has [fallen] from him": "He scarce could tell where his being ended or the world began nor did he care. He lay on his back in the gravel, the earth's core sucking his bones, a moment's giddy vertigo with this illusion of falling outward through blue and windy space, over the offside of the planet, hurtling through the high thin cirrus" (p. 286).

Suttree is not compelled to brood upon the meaning of this sensation. It is the essence of his experience. The suspension or disintegration of identity that he and Harrogate experience is not the same thing as death but is like death in being a different effect of the same process; both real death and this radical decentering of the ego have a common source in the world's disinterested authority over individual being. Early in the novel, Suttree has watched a drowned man's body being grapple-hooked from the river. He passes close enough to the body when it is laid out to notice that the man had on yellow socks and was wearing "his watch on the inside of his wrist as some folks do or used to," and he then observes "with a feeling he could not name that the dead man's watch was still running" (p. 10). The details of the passage speak eloquently for themselves: a particular human being, with funny socks and wristwatch worn on the wrong side, has passed over forever into impersonality, and what was *his* watch is now simply all of time surviving him, as it does all. This wristwatch reports only another version of the same truth. Time is of the world, too, like death, and has no designs upon us flowing past, not even punishment; nor does it call us into question. We call ourselves into question thinking of it, watching a man's watch suddenly become mere time.

Suttree's obsession with time comes naturally to him. At one point he recalls from his childhood watching a racehorse one morning laboring swiftly past him at the rail and hearing the old man beside him "snap his thumb from the keys of the stopwatch" and say with satisfaction "that they had witnessed a thing against which time would not prevail" (p. 136). The remark goes into the boy Suttree's brain the wrong way:

> He meant a thing to be remembered, but the young apostate by the rail at his elbow had already begun to sicken at the slow seeping of life. He could see the shape of the skull through the old man's flesh. Hear sand in the glass. Lives running out like something foul, nightsoil from a cesspipe, a measured dripping in the dark. The clock has run, the horse has run, and which has measured which? (p. 136)

Suttree has been indentured to death from the beginning of his life. He was born one of a pair of identical twins, and his brother had died at birth. The dead brother is the other Suttree, a metaphor that implies that for all of us there is always one of each.

> Mirror image. Gauche carbon. He lies in Woodlawn, whatever be left of the child with whom you shared your mother's belly. He neither spoke nor saw nor does he now. Perhaps his skull held seawater. Born dead and witless both or a terratoma grisly in form. No, for we were like to the last hair. I followed him into the world, me. A breech birth. Hind end fore in common with whales and bats, life forms meant for other mediums than the earth and having no affinity for it. And used to pray for his soul days past. Believing this ghastly circus reconvened elsewhere for alltime. He in the limbo of the Christless righteous, I in a terrestrial hell. (p. 14)

Suttree is obsessed throughout the novel with his macabre connection to this twin, who remains alive in his thoughts and therefore *as if* alive in death's separate kingdom. This in turn has the effect of positing death as a vaguely existent entity ruling a dream world that is different from ours but also always present in it. Suttree's deepest fears have a rational source but present themselves to consciousness in the most primitive idiom of superstition. He thinks *for* the culture he has adopted as well as within it.

Intellectually, of course, Suttree is the antithesis of Harrogate, his unreflective and freewheeling protégé; and he is paralyzingly aware of everything that Harrogate's industry and simplicity shield him from: the true horror of death; the sure corruption and end of friends, love, and all singular things; the impersonal relentlessness of time; the cruel absence of God from the world; the arbitrariness and inconsequentiality of identity in the face of all that. His watchful detachment, however, is so unpurposeful that he seems at times to be no more than a structural device. Yet he is the brain of the book that for good reason bears his name, and all of its lurid idiomatic excesses are his, products of his sinister enchantment and his rejection of the tamed and bloodless order of the middle class in favor of a dangerous reality that speaks and means in all dimensions, never permitting anything to be taken for granted.

One of the effects of Suttree's removing himself from normal society is that it removes him from the ordinary amenities of the modern world and thus in a sense displaces him in time. He is therefore in the presence of death daily in the way a citizen of an earlier century would be. He is not sealed off epistemologically from the always fundamentally threatened status of human nature. People suffer and die before his eyes. One stranger even dies and decomposes in his own bed. Death is not tucked away discreetly in the chambers of hospitals or cosmetically transformed in funeral homes, an offense, as Jacques Aries has argued, against the modern dream of secular happiness. In Suttree's world, on the contrary, death is a crude, apparent fact that has odor and texture. His own life is threatened at one point by a virtually extinct disease: typhoid fever. He is driven, without wholly comprehending why, to fill his son's grave, shoveling dirt until nightfall, fending off the disinterested professionals who wait to supply closure with their tractor and frontloader.

And *being* dead is not at issue. Suttree has flirted with the choice of suicide, understood as ceasing with no pain. In the cemetery where his son is buried he thinks of the dead in the older vaults who are now probably no longer even bones or dust. "How surely are the dead beyond death. Death is what the living carry with them. A state of dread, like some uncanny foretaste of a bitter memory. But the dead do not remember and nothingness is not a curse. Far from it" (p. 153). Death's role in *Suttree* is to be real as a fact and as an idea—not as a state—and in both forms to subvert radically human illusions of security and teleology, as with Harrogate briefly in the caves. The assured counsel of Suttree's father has it exactly backwards: "The world is run by those willing to take the responsibility for the running of it. If it is life that you feel you are missing I can tell you where to find it. In the law courts, in business, in government. There is nothing occurring in the streets. Nothing but a dumb show composed of the helpless and the impotent" (p. 14). Suttree's father has clearly not let the thing in.

The real elders among the impotent and helpless in Suttree's streets, being old and close to death, brood upon death; they recoil from it in anger and bitterness and yet indirectly speak for it. They have lived long enough to understand that the gratifications of power are an illusion. The most obsessive of these ancients is the crazed evangelist who from a high room in his house guards the access to the houseboat community on the river below. At the descent from the bridge he hurls invective down on all who pass. He conceives himself to be the representative of a Christian gospel, but he speaks really for death; and the God he invokes is the God of death. "This viperous evangelist reared up, his elbows cocked and goat's eyes smoking, and thrust a bony finger down. Die! he screamed. Perish a terrible death with thy bowels blown open and black blood boiling from thy nether eye, God save your soul amen" (p. 106). ("Shit fire, said Harrogate, scurrying down the path with one hand over his head.") He is crippled ("They has to carry out his slops and everything" [p. 111]) and is said to have castrated himself. ("Trimmed himself. With a razor. Just sliced em on off honey, what they tell me. That wouldn't cripple you. It would smart some, said Oceanfrog. He was done crippled fore he done it" [p. 111].) He is at once a demented Origen and an untiring Thersites, denying life, embracing death, foresaying doom.

But even with his derangement he is more continuous with the actual world than Suttree's father, naïvely absolutizing the shibboleths of human institutions. Suttree grudgingly admires the old street preachers he meets daily on the corners of McAnally Flats, reflecting that they harangue the "lost world with a vigor unknown to the sane" (p. 66). The not-sane in this reading are closer to death and therefore to truth because death's world is the very inversion of sanity. Suttree's old friend the rag collector speaks for death and the indifference of death's world when he asks Suttree, who will one day come and find him dead, to pour coal oil on him and then burn him on the spot. He says he always figured that there was a God; "I just never did like him" (p. 147). He is ready for death, he says, for after death, "Dont nothin happen. You're dead." Suttree reminds him that he had said before that he believed in God.

> Maybe, he said. I got no reason to think he believes in me. Oh I'd like to see him for a minute if I could.
> What would you say to him?
> Well, I think I'd just tell him. I'd say: Wait a minute. Wait just one minute before you start in on me. Before you say anything, there's just one thing I'd like to know. And he'll say: What's that? And then I'm goin to ast him: What did you have me in that crapgame down there for anyway? I couldnt put any part of it together.
> Suttree smiled. What do you think he'll say?

> The ragpicker spat and wiped his mouth. I dont believe he can answer it, he said, I dont believe there is a answer. (p. 258)

Suttree later goes to visit his sweetly sane Aunt Alice in the home for the insane to which she has been abandoned. She tells him some family history that seems to her now, having outlived all but a few of her kin, a procession of random births and unexpected deaths. "They was nine of us you know. Me and Elizabeth outlived all the boys and now she's gone and I'm in the crazy house. Sometimes I dont know what people's lives are for" (p. 433). Each of these elders, embittered or mystified at the end by the sum of their experience, supposed by the young to provide wisdom and peace, confirms Suttree's experience with his grandfather, whom he perceived to have been filled with uncertainty at the end; and they show how it is meant that the dead wish to take us with them—not into death itself but over into its world in the mind, from which few, apparently, return.

Suttree's waking nightmares are haunted also with progressing intensity by an old crone, Mother She, a geechee witch, whom he seems to meet daily in the streets. Suttree has not had good luck with his near-death experiences, either vicarious or direct. For example, when the old ragman does in fact die, it is Suttree who discovers the body; and he remembers sadly the old man's vow to have a showdown with God to demand some explanations. "Did you ask?" he says to the old man, looking down upon him, in bed with his shoes on, "About the crapgame?" and then adds, as if realizing the real poignancy of figurative thought and speech, "There's no one to ask is there? There's no . . ."—and then stops and leaves.

Near death himself on at least two occasions, his vision at the portal is essentially the same each time. The first time he is hit on the head with a floor buffer in a tavern brawl.

> He swayed. He took a small step, stiffly fending. What waited was not the black of nothing but a foul hag with naked gums smiling and there was no madonna of desire or mother of eternal attendance beyond the dark rain with lamps against the night, the softly cloven powdered breasts and the fragile claviclebones alabastrine above the rich velvet of her gown. The old crone swayed as if to mock him. What man is such a coward he would not rather fall once than remain forever tottering? (p. 187)

Later, in the feverish throes of typhoid, he looks up into the face of his nurse, who is struggling to help him revive, and her face suddenly crumbles away grayly into "a dusty hag's mask." He falls back into his bed sheets, which, wet with sweat, cling to him "like windings" (p. 459). This generic hag of his dreams is the messenger of his reality, the mocker of sweet expectations, the nourishing mother become monsterlike, the sweet grandmother of the Grimms' tale who becomes a devouring wolf. She is also the evil warning of suppressed sexual fear that associates woman with biological imperatives and biology with the curse of death. The latter meaning could hardly be made more explicit than in her appearance in the form of *vagina dentata*: "Out of a pinwheel of brown taffy his medusa beckoned. A gross dancer with a sallow puckered belly, hands cupping a pudendum grown with mossgreen hair, a virid merkin out of which her wet mauve petals smiled and bared from hiding little rows of rubber teeth like the serried jaws of conchshells" (p. 449).

This figure of his nightmares is embodied in his waking world by sinister Mother She, the eerie apotheosis of all the other elders, who has elevated morbidity to a malignant art. She is Ab Jones's folk healer and surgeon, but she also casts evil spells upon enemies. "She has bored a keep in a treebole and hid therein the dung of her enemy and plugged it shut with an oakwood bung. She leans to them in terrible confidence: His guts swoll like a blowed dog. He couldnt get no relief. His stool riz up in his neck till he choken on it and he turn black in the face and his guts bust open and he die a horrible death a screamin and floppin in his own mess" (pp. 280–81). She reads dark fortunes in the arrangement of magical signs recovered from death: "toad and bird bones, yellow teeth, frail shapes of ivory strange or nameless, a small black heart dried hard as stone . . . a joint from a snake's spine, the ribs curved like claws . . . a bat's skull with needleteeth agrin" (p. 281). When Suttree passes her in the street, she does not look at him or speak, but he can smell her as she passes, "a stale musty odor, dusty dry" like that of "violated graves." Her antique teeth are "like seedcorn," and in her "adder's eyes" the sun is reflected split (p. 282). Her tiny hands are "mummied" like those Suttree remembers having seen "crossed on the breast of a dead slave in a wormfluted barrow at the rear of a secondhand furniture store" (p. 423). With her "ageblackened" leather box of sorcerer's effects she reminds Suttree of "a priest with his deathbed kit" (p. 423). She shows Suttree a picture taken of her ancient grandmother with all her relatives after she is dead, someone behind her holding her head up and her sightless eyes toward the camera: "They kep her in a rootcellar till they could fetch the man to come and take the picture." In the picture Mother She is not visible. "I was there when it was took but I never came out." In the "dead place" where she would have been is only a "greyed-out patch, a ghost in the photo of her pellagrous predecessors" (p. 279).

In the course of things Suttree puts himself under this woman's power. It is not clear why, but the encounter seems obligatory, the issue of it a lurid culmination of all of the images and intimations of death that precede and follow. The old woman drugs Suttree with a potion. Then, when he is reeling through hallucinations while lying helpless on her cot, she seems to set upon him, stripping away his clothes and her own and climbing astride him, "the black and shriveled leather teats like empty purses hanging, the thin and razorous palings of the ribs wherein hung a heart yet darker. . . . Black faltress, portress of hellgate. None so ready as she."

> Dry wattled nether lips hung from out the side of her torn stained drawers. Her thighs spread with a sound of rending ligaments, dry bones dragging in their sockets. Her shriveled cunt puckered open like a mouth gawping. He flailed bonelessly in the grip of a ghast black succubus, he screamed a dry and soundless scream. In the pale reach of firelight on the ceiling spiders were clambering toward the cracks in the high corners of the room and his spine was sucked from his flesh and fell clattering to the floor like a jointed china snake. (p. 427)

The effect of this image of his end is to show Suttree to himself simultaneously unmanned and dehumanized, turned grotesquely invertebrate. But then a strange sort of peace ensues for him, unexpectedly, and he drifts in a haze through a series of quite literal childhood memories, as if he were moving backward in time. When he returns later to his houseboat, he seems to himself to be "floating like the first germ of life adrift on the earth's cooling seas" with "all creation yet to come" (p. 430). Oddly, he has passed through death once again to be reborn. His body has been taken and rearranged; his self remains. This ritual encounter and others like it harden him bit by bit against fear, against being overcome by the world of which Mother She is one predatory incarnation. It is not his last engagement with death, nor his worst; the ravages of his illness impend. But the imagery here is as lurid as it will be, and as primal, and includes the passing of the sexual nightmare. The specter of Mother She is purged—at that very moment, in fact; she does not appear as herself again. It is after this, too, that in no doubt unconscious stages Suttree begins to transcend the river, as he does in the end for good, leaving behind him the corpse of an unknown dead man in his bed.

The whole episode with the old woman is reported with such solemn extravagance, and she herself is so preposterously arcane, that it is hard to know whether we are supposed to take the occasion seriously—especially given the faint implication that the old woman's behavior all along has been an elaborate scheme designed simply to get Suttree into bed. Certainly it is hard to know from it where reality leaves off and fantasy begins. But whether or not on the surface the episode is intended seriously, there is woven into it a faint allegorical pattern that repeats the pattern of Suttree's life. If we think of the old woman, as Suttree thinks of her, as an agent of death, possessing supernatural intelligence and powers—rather than as the charlatan she must in fact be—then when she says to him, "To know what will come is the same as to make it so" (p. 423), it means something. It is a version of the admonition in the opening pages about the thing unknown: "he is not to be dwelt upon for it is by just suchwise that he's invited in" (p. 5). And when Suttree asks, after the spell has taken hold, "Should I go home?" and she answers, "It don't make no difference where you go" (p. 425), she has described to him in plain truth his biological and psychoanalytical bondage to death.

Suttree's voluntary passiveness is emphasized throughout the episode, and this in itself reflects his way of living in the presence of death in the ordinary world. The drug also induces an exaggerated illusion of watchful detachment: "Suddenly he realized that this scene was past and he was looking at its fading reality like a watcher from another room. Then he was watching the watcher" (p. 426). When Suttree struggles to raise himself from the cot, he is "unsure as to whether he should walk about. There seemed no purpose to it" (p. 425). The dead would take us with them if they could, and the conflict with them is reenacted repeatedly, giving the novel its structure and its point. But to acknowledge the impoverishment of the self, of the "subject," in the presence of the blank other is paradoxically to be strengthened.

The fact that Suttree comes through such experiences as this one suggests that his capacity to survive despair and disintegration of the ego is as much systemic and preconscious as it is an act of conscious will and that it somehow automatically reasserts itself when needed—a kind of biological miracle like the blood clotting to seal off a wound instead of simply flowing on, as seems more natural. This inborn power would be the source, too, of Ab's incongruous ability to contrive dignity and strength. It suggests a secular internalization of the Christian mystery of death and resurrection, and over the span of the novel this adaptation becomes *the* human meaning in existence.

We might infer, too, that the associated emphasis upon this notably intransitive affirmation is a surviving influence in Suttree of his Roman Catholic training—though it may be argued ultimately that the church itself merely institutionalizes a primordial desire of the human for what is absent from being. The struggle with death in *Suttree* is a conflict between unmediated fact and mediated value. That struggle is antecedent to all other philosophical considerations, since any other philosophical discussion must begin with the conflict resolved on behalf of value. It is because of the elemental nature of this contest that *Suttree* seems so oddly like a novel of ideas in which ideas are not even meditated upon or discussed. "First things first" seems to be the ruling intellectual principle, and first things in this respect are prior to abstraction.

The very fundamental and therefore pervasive nature of this conflict creates the tension that makes the novel work intellectually—that makes it *do* work at every interval. There is no point at which that pressure is suspended, for the point of it is that experience is a sustained dialectical striving and can be transcended, albeit marginally, only when the principle is understood and endorsed. One goes on from there—Suttree does so at any rate—knowing that resolution is not possible and that dreaming of it is flight. The dialectic is not Hegelian—that is, teleological. It is self-contained. Events and images confirm it, leaving discourse extraneous.

This theme is not presented discursively, but it is often focused for us suddenly and sharply by episodes that keep us from losing track of what is at stake in the otherwise elliptical and seemingly random organization of events. In the space of less than a hundred pages, three instances occur. The first takes place during an aimless journey Suttree takes down the river on a hot Sunday afternoon, which eventually brings him to the scene of a peaceful baptism. He engages in idle talk with two of the participants about being saved and about the unbridgeable difference between mere "sprinklin" on the one hand and "total nursin" on the other. ("It won't take if you don't get total nursin," says one of the old men watching, a lay preacher. "That old sprinklin business won't get it, buddy boy.... I'd rather just to go on and be infidel as that" [p. 122].) They watch two congregation members being immersed, one a girl who arises smiling, the other an older man who is frightened and struggles and makes an amusing spectacle for the onlookers. Suttree is urged to go on and be saved but declines: "Suttree knew the river well already." The whole episode is appealingly friendly and sociable, and standing alone it might be construed as a provisional endorsement of faith.

But the episode does not stand alone. It is opposed and balanced by Suttree's having remembered a few moments earlier being near the same spot when he was a child and being instructed in killing by an old turtle hunter, watching a turtle's skull being blown away "in a cloud of brainpulp and bonemeal" and the "wrinkled empty skin" suddenly hanging "from the neck like a torn sock" (p. 118). This is the hunter who reappears in the nightmare later with his terrifying "turkles." Turtles themselves recur in the narration, grotesquely vivid, as here, primordial reminders of what we otherwise choose to forget. The river of blown-up turtles and the river of being saved are both real, but they cannot be reconciled to each other in the mind. The two episodes form a definitive and representative tension. This tension or negative dialectic seems to link up with the odd twinning motif that pervades the novel.

Weeks after the day on the river Suttree learns that his son has died, and he makes his way by bus to the town where the boy is to be buried. He is set upon there by his dazed and grieving in-laws when he goes to see his estranged wife. He later watches the funeral from a place apart, cut and bruised, grieving beyond thought. As the child is commended to the earth—by strangers, it is noted—the mother cries out suddenly and sinks to the ground and is "lifted up and helped away wailing." "Stabat Mater Dolorosa," Suttree remembers from mass, associating mortal experience with the way of the cross. But then in the next instant he remembers his wife when she was young, remembers "her hair in the morning before it was pinned, black, rampant, savage with loveliness. As if she slept in perpetual storm"; and Suttree goes "to his knees in the grass, his hands cupped over his ears"—as much to shut out the hair as the wailing, tormented by the contradictions of death and the promise of love. He finds release after this burning revelation is over by filling his son's grave, but the point is indelibly imprinted for him, with others like it, on the crude palimpsest of memory and experience. It is meant to be imprinted for us as well so as to associate with other such small but resonating subject rhymes that make the narrative cohere.

One other powerful version of this dialectic mystery is related to Suttree by his older friend, Daddy Watson, who has called it up from his own sustaining memory store. Daddy Watson, an old railroad man, has hung on in a way that the old ragman has not. His memories are generously vivid and keep life churning, in motion for him. He tells Suttree a simple story that charismatically restates again the hidden text. Suttree has asked him how he has happened to end up here in his shack in the slum, much like Suttree's. "I aint ended yet," he replies.

> Used to hobo a right smart. Back in the thirties. They wasnt no work I dont care what you could do. I was ridin through the mountains one night, state of Colorado. Dead of winter it was and bitter cold. I had just a smidgin of tobacco, bout enough for one or two smokes. I was in one of them old slatsided cars and I'd been up and down in it like a dog tryin to find some place where the wind wouldnt blow. Directly I scrunched up in a corner and rolled me a smoke and lit it and thowed the match down. Well, they was some sort of stuff in the floor about like tinder and it caught fire. I jumped up and stomped on it and it aint done nothin but burn faster. Wasnt two minutes the whole car was afire. I run to the door and got it open and we was goin up this grade through the mountains in the snow with the moon on it and it was just blue lookin and dead quiet out there and them big old black pine trees goin by. I jumped for it and lit in a snowbank and what I'm goin to tell you you'll think peculiar but it's the god's truth. That was in nineteen and thirty-one and if I live to be a hunnerd year old I dont think I'll ever see anything as pretty as that train on fire goin up that mountain and around the bend and them flames lightin up the snow and the trees and the night. (p. 182)

This could not seem *very* peculiar to Suttree, since it is the minimal point of his experience—the God's truth—that we dwell inescapably in paradox and should learn, as Daddy Watson has, to be willing to do so, since things could be a great deal worse. Yet even Daddy Watson goes down in the end. He disappears. Then, on the day Suttree visits the mental hospital to see his Aunt Alice, he notices as he leaves "an old man in a striped railroader's hat . . . holding a huge watch in his hand and following Suttree with his eyes as if he'd time him" (p. 433). It is Daddy Watson. Their eyes meet, but Suttree cannot say his name. His robust crankiness has waned; he is passing over slowly into the generic world where names no longer matter.

The novel is as rich in these oblique paradigms as it is in characters, and they show us collectively how it is that Suttree's innate will to affirm seems perpetually at risk and difficult to sustain and nourish. In the dialectic of being, each moment or principle, each act, has definition only in an ironic and threatened form, just as Suttree has a dead form in his infant twin brother. There is no unironic alternative and no metaphysical court of appeals. Suttree's hard lessons harden him and eventually free him from sentimental regret, leaving him with perspective, which is at least *like* transcendence.

The hardest lessons come to him through the intercession of the two women he loves in the course of his story; he permits himself the lapse of believing each to offer, in her uncomplicated love for him, a way of escape. His relationship with each one, touching and erotic and conventional in a recognizably American way, turns out only to confirm the paradigm rather than overriding it. With Wanda, his friend Reese's daughter, Suttree is drawn under the spell of an uncomplicated sexual innocence and is therefore freed temporarily from his habitual anxiety. Wanda is not old enough to know or care about the true character of the world. She is unequivocally giving, a restored, avid promise of sexuality and youth. In the beginning, at the remote encampment on the river where the Reeses gather mussels, the dark universe itself is exposed for Suttree each night in its enormity, unmediated by human settlement. Gathered around the campfire in this darkness, sharing their sparse provisions, Reese and his family are "subdued" and the wife bitter and apprehensive, "as if an order had been imposed upon them from without" (p. 348). Suttree lies awake in this scary place watching the heavens "locked and wheeling" (p. 354). But Wanda, without effort or words, tames the world for Suttree in the brief interval of their furtive, salacious time together. "With his ear to the womb of this child he could hear the hiss of meteorites through the blind stellar depths" (p. 358); and when he is alone in the aftermaths, he is struck, uncharacteristically, by the "fidelity of the earth he inhabited," and he bears it "a sudden love" (p. 354).

But then one day two twin brothers, possum hunters, come into their camp. They are like the theme of the novel displaced into a ludicrous dream form. They are so nearly identical that they themselves forget which one is which, have broken arms at distant places at the same time, communicate telepathically. To demonstrate this mystery to the skeptics, one of the twins whispers a word into Reese's ear that the other is to guess. The word is *brother*; and as Vernon and Fernon hoot maniacally at the others' astonishment when the second twin guesses right. Suttree is chilled at the thought that his own twin has communicated with him, one of the temporarily forgotten dead reporting in.

Late that night the summer rains return and the slate wall above the camp disintegrates and collapses, crushing Wanda beneath it. The "Stabat Mater" refrain recurs. Suttree hears Mrs. Reese in the darkness crying out to God, meaning for Him to answer, Suttree thinks, with a sickness of heart; and a flash of lightning reveals a "baroque pieta, the woman gibbering and kneeling in the rain clutching at sheared limbs and rags of meat among the slabs of rock" (p. 362). The paradigm has run its course again, as if "locked and wheeling" like the stars. Suttree leaves that night, rowing downriver, Wanda's dark blood crusted on his hands. "He was a man with no plans for going back the way he'd come nor telling any soul at all what he had seen" (p. 363).

When several months later Suttree becomes the paramour of a clever prostitute named Joyce, an illusion of déjà vu permeates the entire episode, as if Wanda had slipped back into the world through a hole in time, grown-up and stouter and wiser in the ways of the world, though every bit as doomed. Her doom takes a different form, but it is there from the start; and in the end it is just as enigmatically random. In its early stages the relationship of Suttree and Joyce is voluptuous and childlike. Joyce is vigorous, cheerfully lewd, prospering in her trade. She is pleased to be able to provide Suttree with spiffy clothes, comfortable quarters, and days of dreamy lassitude. Together they are impulsive and improvident, going on long cab rides in the winter to see the mountains in the snow and formations in the trees and in the mouths of caves. Joyce "looking out with child's eyes at this wonderland" says, "It's fucking beautiful" (p. 399). They drink whiskey chilled with icicles, make love beneath the blanket in the back seat of a cab.

But by the time summer comes, the enchantment has begun to dissipate in barely registered stages. Unaccountably one day Suttree faces himself in the mirror and poses to see how he would look in death. Bouts of drunkenness increase. Climbing the stairway to their rooms, Suttree reobserves details that speak of a different order of things: a "light in the ceiling thirty feet above like some dim nebula viewed from the pit," an "inexplicable picture in a gilt frame," "two birds composed of actual feathers dyed bizarrely like hats and defying forever the orders of taxonomy," down the hallway "the door with no name where he lived" (p. 405).

Odd, unremarked-upon associations with Wanda assert themselves at intervals. From his window in the "darkening eve" he watches the city's "wandlike lights come up" (p. 404). At a lake they visit he fetches up from the "bonewhite driftwood" on the bared shoreline a "huge blue mussel shell wasted paper thin" (p. 408) and gives it to Joyce, who carries it carefully, cradling inside it an arrowhead they have found and a strange pebble that resembles an eye. Loneliness pervades this setting in the exposed tree stumps and their twisted roots casting shadows on the water, the gulls rising from the sandbar and drifting away in the late afternoon sunlight, even as Joyce kneels beside Suttree and nibbles his ear, rests her breast upon his arm. After Joyce and Suttree have fought and separated, Suttree reads in the paper one day about a young girl's body found buried under trash.

And so the end comes. They have bought a fine car and driven to an exclusive resort in Asheville to pose humorously as people of means, acting out a parody of middle-class marriage. Then one Sunday, unaccountably, Joyce is seized by a fit of violent grief. She begins destroying the fine car from the inside, stripping the gears into reverse, smashing the radio, and suddenly shattering the windshield and kicking it out into the street. "It's just a car," she says to Suttree when he protests, defining for the novel this appalling, authentic difference between cars and lives: "It can be fixed" (p. 410). The money she carries with her she begins to tear into shreds in great wads to fling them from the window, making again the same point: "this money would never do anybody any good" (p. 411). It is the end, of course, closure of the circle. The shattered windshield and the shredded money are not broken, fallen pieces of rock and slabs of shale; but they are associated mysteriously with the violence of Wanda's death, especially two pages later, when Suttree reads about the girl buried under trash. The end with Joyce has come as abruptly and as randomly as Wanda's end, though in this case it is because of knowledge of the world rather than despite sweet ignorance of it, an unsuppressible prophecy fulfilling itself, consciousness infiltrated by the world, another way the dead have of taking us with them.

On one of their last outings together before the sudden end, Suttree and Joyce sit on a hill at night, looking down upon the fairgrounds below. Suttree is moved to wonder if Joyce had ever been "a child at a fair dazed by the constellations of light and the hurdygurdy music of the merrygoround and the raucous calls of the barkers. Who saw in all that shoddy world a vision that a child's grace knows and never the sweat and the bad teeth and the nameless stains in the sawdust, the flies and the stale delirium and the vacant look of solitaries who go among these garish holdings seeking a thing they could not name" (p. 409). His answer comes as they watch the fireworks go up—"glass flowers exploding . . . slow trails of color down the sky like stains dispersing in the sea"—and he turns to her to find her crying without knowing why; and below them suddenly the city seems "frozen in a blue void" (p. 409).

The metaphor of the carnival conceals a dialectical transaction too; it therefore remains central and recurs. Even Joyce knows this, and it transpires that her own sexuality is such a way of coming unstuck in time and returning: "In the toils of orgasm—she said, she said—she'd be whelmed in a warm green sea through which, dulled by the murk of it, pass a series of small suns like the footlights of a revolving stage, an electric carousel wheeling in a green ether" (p. 415). When Suttree goes to his son's funeral, the only memory he can call up clearly is (*of course*, he might also have thought) the ironic one. "All night he'd tried to see the child's face in his mind but he could not. All he could remember was the tiny hand in his as they went to the carnival fair and a fleeting image of elf's eyes wonderstruck at the wide world in its wheeling. Where a ferriswheel swung in the night and painted girls were dancing and skyrockets went aloft and broke to shed a harlequin light above the fairgrounds and the upturned faces" (p. 150).

Being of different ages, Wanda and Joyce are at the two poles of the carnival metaphor; so are Suttree and his boy, connected in that memory at the hands. But the metaphor also grows complicated. During Suttree's strange hermit's sojourn in the mountains, he has a vision one night, in the wake of a storm, of a carnival procession from, it seems, an unknown medieval time, "a troupe of squalid merrymakers bearing a caged wivern on shoulderpoles and other alchemical game, chimeras and cacodemons skewered up on boarspears and a pharmacopoeia of hellish condiments adorning a trestle and toted by trolls with an eldern gnome for guidon . . . a piper who piped a pipe of ploverbone. . . . A tattered gonfalon embroidered with stars now extinct. Nemoral halfworld inhabitants, figures in buffoon's motley" (p. 287).

The language itself is carnivalesque: dense, tumultuous, and fleshy. The materiality of the world speaks in the cacophony of the style. The festival itself proclaims, he sees, "the perishability of his flesh," a celebration from within of the grotesqueness of mortality. The traditional etymology of *carnival*—"farewell to the flesh" (*carne vale*)—has come into play from the archives of Suttree's Catholic training, but the season of Lent that this carnival precedes is one not of spiritual renewal but of death and the void. In other words, either affirmation arises in the midst of death or death prevails before its time. The world aloft in the lights and exploding flowers of fireworks is not separate from but one with the world below, where "solitaries" wander, "seeking a thing they could not name."

Suttree's ordinary life and surroundings are not much different from this bizarre procession—among his friends, with their drunken revelry, raucous conviviality, comical names, and outlandish costumes. Suttree and his friend Blind Richard are drinking one day at Ab Jones's place. Suttree has explained to Richard that the tables they are drinking off of are really tombstones recovered from an island flooded by a dam project. Richard is uneasy about this, even as he reads for Suttree the names on the underside. They talk it out.

> We ought not to be doin this. Drinkin off folks's gravestones.
> Why not?
> I dont know.
> Would you care?
> If it was some of my kin I would.
> What if it was you?
> I aint dead.
> If you were dead. And me and Callahan drank off it. Your stone.
> I dont know. I'd be dead. I'd drink off Billy Ray's.
> I would too, said Suttree.
> I'd drink off of it in a minute.
> Suttree grinned.
> Course maybe if you was dead you'd think different. I mean, if you're dead and all why I expect you got to be pretty religious.
> We'd drink you a toast. Have a good time.
> Richard smiled wanly. Well, he said. I like a good time well as the next feller.
> I'll get us another beer. (pp. 369–70)

The carnival spirit approaches ideology, though it is never serious enough to be called that. It is closer to ritual, and the many shared beers in the novel (Richard insists on buying this round) are like demystified sacraments. The point is brought home here when the next name Blind Richard deciphers is William Callahan, the same as that of their brawling Irish friend who is shortly afterwards killed. It is necessarily in the spirit of carnival, its truths being unevadable, that Suttree is able to affirm his existence.

Suttree's ironic idealism is evident from the beginning in his nostalgic though vague identification with the church. That association is pervasive in the style of the novel as well, in the subliminal form of imagery and idiom that continually links the sacred and profane. Many of these signs are overt. Early in the novel, in his aimless prowls through the netherworld of Knoxville at night, Suttree sometimes watches the services in Negro meetinghouses from outside and, a "pale pagan" sitting on the curb, listens to the gospel music issuing forth. One night he intercepts a radio broadcast in his tooth fillings: "He was stayed in a peace that drained his mind, for even a false adumbration of the world of the spirit is better than none at all" (p. 21). On the Monday mornings when he stands listening to the demented street preachers in the market, he is listening "for some stray scrap of news from beyond the pale" (p. 66). He worries when Leonard is eager to shove his dead chained father into the dark river—"Shit, this'll take his ass to the bottom like a fucking rocket"—without first saying a few words (p. 251). Leonard says that his father had never been to church, and Suttree replies, "All the more reason." Since the only words Suttree knows are Catholic ones and the father was clearly no Catholic, they end up doing nothing, though Leonard, garbling the text, does suggest reciting "that part that goes through the shadow of the valley of death" (p. 251).

Drunkenly, one night not long after this, Suttree wanders into the Church of the Immaculate Conception. ("The virtues of a stainless birth were not lost on him" [p. 253].) This is the church of his childhood, and memories press forward; but there is nothing here for him but grimness and gothic remonstrance—recollections of the terror of sin, the "deathreek of the dark and half scorched muslin" of the priests' visions of hell, tireless "orthopedic moralizing": "Lives proscribed and doom in store, doom's adumbration in the smoky censer" (p. 254). A priest wakens him when he dozes off and admonishes him for sleeping in God's house. "It's not God's house," Suttree says, not meaning at this point, necessarily, that God has no house, only that this one, of death and oppression, is not it. After listening one night to the singing from the Grand Avenue Mission—revelers caroling "perhaps perverse and secret deities"—he goes back to his old parochial school, where he had learned his share of "christian witchcraft" (p.

304). A priest in the shadows watches him wander through the abandoned building. When Suttree looks back after he leaves, the priest is observing him from an upstairs window. Suttree sees "a catatonic shaman . . . sealed in glass" (p. 305).

In these wanderings Suttree is not unlike the "solitaries" he has remembered seeing at carnivals, going among "these garish holdings seeking a thing they could not name" (p. 409). He seeks unhopefully to rediscover the "lost world" (p. 50) that is now darkened everywhere by the "shadow of the valley of death" and it seems, as he reconstructs his past, that is was never there to begin with.

The surviving memories of Suttree's experience of redemption, of the hope of providential rescue, might be argued, as a kind of irreversible conditioning, to account for his inability to succumb to death's world absolutely, to explain what is left of a saving, steadying idealism in his failing constitution. It could also, and as easily, be imagined to have made his situation worse, since "false adumbrations of the world of spirit" can be mockeries that sharpen the suffering in reality because of the grim contrast.

But the intersection of two worlds is undeniably constant and has—to carry forward the phrase from *Outer Dark*—the redundancy of a dream. Where it does not move him to fruitless, nostalgic pilgrimages, it thoroughly infiltrates his and our way of perceiving his world. This infiltration creates a pattern in the metaphorical texture of the narrative that is in itself dialectical and that also merges with, to reinforce, the larger dialectical structure of the novel's reality, making it more deeply continuous and coherent.

Intimations can flourish in the most unlikely moments. Against a "squalid winter sky" smokestacks of the city rise like "gothic organpipes" (p. 383). A procession of car lights on the highway one night seems like "the candles of acolytes" (p. 348). A girl who has been gang-raped wakes in the morning to see two Negro boys perched watching her on the fenders of the car like "gibbons purloined from the architraves of an old world cathedral" (p. 416). Even one of Harrogate's poisoned bats falls from the air onto Suttree's tin roof with "a mild and vesperal bong" (p. 214). In the woods of the mountains, snow expires on the filthy cuff of Suttree's clothes like "a delicate host" (p. 289). An old man in a wheelchair cringing by the wall in Aunt Alice's ward seems to be chanting to himself "some silent doxology" (p. 432). Some images are less oxymoronic but remain suggestive. Wanda with her head down in embarrassment at the table at the Reeses' encampment seems "to be at grace" (p. 349). Blind Richard comes one night to the bridge, calling in the darkness to Suttree to come help him down to the river. Suttree sees him raising "his thin arm into the lamplight like a supplicant to the chalice of God's bright mercies" (p. 372). For Suttree, embittered and lapsed, none of this points toward a metaphysic; it rather reminds him of the absence of one. He is a hierophant without a theme.

The pressure of meaning in *Suttree* is as haunting and as powerful as it is in *Outer Dark*; and since *Suttree* has a far more sophisticated, questioning protagonist at its center, some kind of release of that pressure seems obligatory to its form—and the release is ultimately achieved. It is achieved, moreover, without violation to the novel's form and character and by a means that, remarkably, leaves the mystery and opaqueness of the world intact while showing that coming to terms with it achieves a common good. Metaphysical resolution is beyond the reach of thought: Suttree comprehends and accepts the terms of this contract. But at least a kind of ontological clarity comes to him in a series of visions that seem also to hold him fast against dying in his feverish struggle with disease. He sees himself, dying, being voided by a vast vagina into a "cold dimension without time without space and where all was motion" (p. 452). An attending priest tells him that for him to have survived, God must have been watching over him. Suttree says, "You would not believe what watches" and then "He is not a thing. Nothing ever stops moving" (p. 461).

This is the simple summary of his understanding—that there is no metaphysical first principle, no foundational truth. It is not so much Heraclitus without Logos as it is Heraclitus with Logos rudely desanctified, for he has this dream too.

> Mr Suttree it is our understanding that at curfew rightly decreed by law and in that hour wherein night draws to its proper close and the new day commences and contrary to conduct befitting a person of your station you betook yourself to various low places within the shire of McAnally and there did squander several ensuing years in the company of thieves, derelicts, miscreants, pariahs, poltroons, spalpeens, curmudgeons, clotpolls, murderers, gamblers, bawds, whores, trulls, brigands, topers, tosspots, sots and archsots, lobcocks, smellsmocks, runagates, rakes, and other assorted and felonious debauchees.
> I was drunk, cried Suttree. Seized in a vision of the archetypal patriarch himself unlocking with enormous keys the gates of Hades. A floodtide of screaming fiends and assassins and thieves and hirsute buggers pours forth

into the universe, tipping it slightly on its galactic axes. The stars go rolling down the void like redhot marbles. These simmering sinners with their cloaks smoking carry the Logos itself from the tabernacle and bear it through the streets while the absolute prebarbaric mathematick of the western world howls them down and shrouds their ragged biblical form in oblivion. (pp. 457–58)

The fiends, assassins, thieves, and hirsute buggers it seems clear are in fact Suttree's friends set loose into the world to wreak upon it what it deserves. The Logos is no longer in the tabernacle but in the streets, in hearts, in the community of the living and dying who thrive close to the raw edge of being, where they are in turn ignored—"shrouded in oblivion"—by those who absolutize their vested interest in a vision of order and sanctity. Even the inspired silliness of some of Suttree's dreams expresses affirmation of a cheerfully nihilistic play.

Suttree has also said to the priest that he has learned in his delirium that "there is one Suttree and one Suttree only" (p. 461). A simple reading would hold this to mean that there is only one Suttree lifespan, complete—like the dialectic—in itself, beginning, then ending, leading nowhere. But Suttree has also put his own name in the place of God's in this parody of catechism, so a deeper reach of understanding may also be implied. After the affair with Joyce has ended so disastrously, Suttree goes back to his houseboat and sets his old life back in order; and one night, settled in finally, he has a silent conversation with himself by way of taking stock. He concedes that he is not unhappy. He asserts that he has learned that the last and first suffer equally; and when the interlocutor self is skeptical, he rephrases his conviction: "It is not alone in the dark of death that all souls are one soul." And he repents of one error: "I spoke with bitterness about my life and I said that I would take my own part against the slander of oblivion and against the monstrous facelessness of it and that I would stand a stone in the very void where all the world would read my name. Of that vanity I recant all" (p. 414). Later, during a break in his fever, he says to an attending nurse, "I know all souls are one soul and all souls lonely" (p. 459). Staying in a friend's house after he has escaped the hospital, he lies awake the first night listening to the sirens in the empty street. "He lay in his chrysalis of gloom and made no sound, share by share sharing his pain with those who lay in their blood by the highwayside or in the floors of glass strewn taverns or manacled in jail" (p. 464). "Even the damned in hell have the community of their suffering," he concludes, and this is a great deal to have, the community of suffering that binds people in their common cause against the rule of death. This commonality within, which may and should arise from the universality of suffering, is the quid pro quo in human life, brought into life, ironically, by death. It is the Logos in the streets, God in his real house, displaced from the tabernacle. The harsh words Suttree has spoken earlier to the dead ragman turn out to be measured words arising from a residual moral and existential stamina: "You have no right to represent people this way.... A man is all men. You have no right to your wretchedness" (p. 422).

Despair is a form of self-pity, and self-pity is both isolation—vanity of kind—and a denial of the responsibility to make and be what is human. There being one Suttree and one Suttree only turns out to mean, then, close to the reverse of what it apears to mean. It is Walt Whitman speaking in a new idiom and time: "A man is all men." Before Suttree leaves the city, at the end, one of his last acts is to divest himself of the lucky charms and amulets he has collected over time—tokens of a fear of deities unknown, of an afterworld—for he has now taken for talisman, it is said, only "the simple human heart within him" (p. 468). The point is made sentimentally, but the sentiment is fitted to the occasion.

McAnally Flats is being torn down, as Suttree leaves, to make room for the new expressway and eventually, beyond the foreknowledge of the novel, ironically, a World's Fair, the advance of the Jaycee vision of human purpose. At the still point of transition, the wreckers have left images for another vision that will stick fast in Suttree's memory: shelled facades, halved houses broken open to the world, old sofas bloating in the rain on cinder lawns, "shriveled tables sloughing off their papery veneers," and "cutaway elevations" eerie and eloquent in the evening light, "little cubicles giving onto space, an iron bedstead, a freestanding stairwell to nowhere" (pp. 463–64). Suttree thinks of the wreckers cynically as "gnostic workmen who would have down this shabby shapeshow that masks the higher world of form." The builders of cities continue to miss the point as they continue the collective doomed flight from nature and death.

Early in the novel—on the occasion of his remembering the old man and the horse and the stopwatch and his first apprehension of the horror of time—Suttree visits an old manor house associated with his youth and fallen now into ruins. He has a strange vision there, standing in the darkened dining hall, of an ancient feast, Saxon warriors gorging meat and hearing in the distance the sounds of hounds bringing a stag to bay. On the board are only water and meat. And as the men listen to the hunters, they wait also for the water-bearer; but "he does not come, and does not come" (p. 136). At the end of the novel, however, the water-bearer does come, as naturally and mysteriously as it is a novelist's gift to imagine; and with him return the hunting dogs.

Water has the same talismanic significance in *Suttree* that it has in *Outer Dark*, though its presence is less exposed in a text so dense with other messages and signs. Suttree, drunk in jail, dreams of cool water. Gene Harrogate, beslimed with sewage in his cave, craves a glass of ice water that he would give ten dollars for, he says, cash money. The waters of the upper reaches of the French Broad River, where Suttree and Wanda are together in their prelapsarian idyll, is so clear as to allow the river bottom to be seen in sharp, sunlit detail, a contrast to Suttree's river home in the city, which is plumbless and murky. Suttree once imagines, enigmatically, that the color of this life is water. He notices the holy water in a scalloped basin in the vestibule of the old church he returns to. He asks for water in the hospital when his fever has abated. Then, as he leaves Knoxville, hitchhiking along the course of the new expressway, he watches a boy bearing water to the road construction crew below him. The incident is beautifully and painstakingly rendered.

> When all these had been attended the boy came down along the edge of the ditch and handed up the dipper to the backhoe operator. Suttree saw him take it and tilt his head and drink and flick the last drops toward the earth and lean down and restore the dipper to the watercarrier. They nodded to each other and the boy turned and looked toward the road. Then he was coming down across the clay and over the ruts and laddered tracks of machinery. His dusty boots left prints across the black macadam and he came up to Suttree where he stood by the roadside and swung the bucket around and brought the dipper up all bright and dripping and offered it. Suttree could see the water beading coldly on the tin and running in tiny rivulets and drops that steamed on the road where they fell. He could see the pale gold hair that lay along the sunburned arms of the waterbearer like new wheat and he beheld himself in wells of smoking cobalt, twinned and dark and deep in child's eyes, blue eyes with no bottoms like the sea. He took the dipper and drank and gave it back. The boy dropped it into the bucket. Suttree wiped his mouth on the back of his hand. Thanks, he said. (pp. 470–71)

Of all the meanings that congregate in this episode—the ritual drinking among the men, the water itself, Suttree seeing himself—*able* to see himself, twinned and renewed in the boy's eyes—the most affecting is the simple unsymbolic fact that the boy has seen this stranger standing in the sun on the side of the road and has climbed up the bank to bring him cold water. Such human things happen routinely and yet, when framed and focused, have the mysterious beauty of sacraments. In fact, in the next instant, a car stops, though Suttree has not lifted a hand, and the driver says, "Let's go." Suttree looks back as they drive away, and where the water boy was has come a lank, enormous hound sniffing at the spot where Suttree has stood. So he remembers the huntsman as well, whose "hounds tire not": "I have seen them in a dream, slaverous and wild and their eyes crazed with ravening for souls in this world. Fly them" (p. 471). These archaic words are the right words for an ancient struggle. All people are in all time's language. They show that Suttree is fully conscious of the two symbolic acts at the end, drinking the water and fleeing the hounds, and that that consciousness is his transcendence—modest by most standards, certainly, but true to his experience and all that his world allows and requires.

It is an appealing measure of McCarthy's commitment to his sense of the real human position in the world that he never permits us to forget that we are solidly there in it instead of in some readerly station just above it in our heads. Even such a privileged transcendence as that he knows to be an infrequent achievement. One of the novelistic rhythms that seems obligatory to him, therefore, is that of a form of democratic recentering, a means by which intellectual pretensions and visionary excesses can be held in check—or, to alter the metaphor, reeled in. By this means, where and how people really live daily in the world becomes the touchstone of any value, the determinant of what is precious and what is not. One memorable instance of this test is the episode in which Suttree comes down finally from his purgational sojourn in the mountains—starved, bearded, filthy from sleeping under leaves, his only garment a ragged blanket, his head full of chimeras—and encounters an obtuse deer hunter in his stand in a tree, one of the race who is belligerently unattuned to metaphysical discourse and pedantic wordplay. A wonderfully comic scene ensues; through it Suttree is grudgingly restored to real life and we are depressurized in order to reenter, gladly, the real world.

Two other incidents like this one, though not funny, occur just before the novel's end; they are both, in different ways, deeply affecting moments at the point in the novel when emotional grounding seems most necessary. Before Suttree starts out of town, he makes a last solemn circuit around his old neighborhood and encounters his garish homosexual friend, John, known mainly by his street name, Trippin Through the Dew. Trippin Through the Dew is one of the number of people in *Suttree* who has drawn a bad hand in life and has contrived bravely, in his outlandish way, to make the most of it. He is black, effeminate, of indeterminate age—perhaps sixty or older—and inexhaustibly buoyant. He has not seen Suttree since the illness and hasn't known about it and is shocked by Suttree's wasted appearance. His solicitude is both evident and genuine. Suttree tells him that he is leaving the city for good, and his friend is at first incredulous and then openly, uninhibitedly grieved. Suddenly all of the carnival bravado, the drag-queen jive, the lurid persona fall away, and there is plain John standing there speaking, sad to be losing yet another friend and street brother, concerned that this friend will not be okay somewhere else. He refuses to believe that Suttree won't be back. He is worried that he needs money. He enjoins Suttree to keep in touch if only with a postcard from time to time. During this exchange each has taken the other's hand, and they stand there holding hands as they talk in the middle of the street. When Trippin Through the Dew is reassured that Suttree is okay, he squeezes his hand and then steps back and gives him "a sort of crazy little salute." "Best luck in the world baby," he says, and Suttree says, "Thanks John, you too" (p. 468); and the scene is gone—though not before its simple relevance seems to have gathered for us all the faces and the sounds of voices of the novel's other living and dead.

Just before this penultimate episode, Gene Harrogate's half sister, Josie, has turned up unexpectedly at Suttree's houseboat, looking for Gene: "A big rawboned woman, her hair matted all over her face. The armpits of her cotton housedress black with sweat" (p. 465). She has had no news of her brother since he left their distant rural home, and she has come to Knoxville to find him and to tell him that their mother has died. Suttree has to tell her that he is in the penitentiary, which she seems to think a normal outcome, given the course of things. He has to explain where the penitentiary is—in Petros—and how to get there on the bus. "They aint fixin to electricate him are they?" she says, and Suttree says no, that he's in for three to five, possibly out in eighteen months. Suttree assures her that Gene is a good boy. She thanks him for being his friend and turns to leave but then stops at the rail.

> What was that name again? she said.
> Brushy Mountain?
> No. That othern you said.
> Petros.
> Petros, she said. She said it again, staring emptily upward. Then she started down the catwalk. There must have been a loose cleat somewhere because going down it she fell. Her feet shot from under her and she sat down. The plank bowed deeply and rose again, lifting her flailing figure. She managed to get a grip and steady herself and she stood carefully and went on, teetering along till she reached the shore.
> Are you all right? called Suttree.
> She didnt look back. She raised one hand and waved it and went on, stooped and heavy gaited, across the fields and the tracks toward the town. (pp. 466–67)

Considering all that we know about her and her life—and we seem to know everything there is from just this brief association—Josie Harrogate's barely articulate stoicism seems to express both hopelessness and hope, and she therefore embodies in this moment the irreducible human value of the entire book. The effect of McCarthy's bringing these two episodes together at the end is to remind readers of how, at a very simpleminded level, existence precedes essence—of how human feeling and the necessary physical action of getting up and going on, putting one step in front of the other, are prior to thought and ideas. It reminds readers how it is that most people in the world, who are not likely to be reading such a novel as *Suttree*, have other things to worry over first: how to make the odd name of a town stick in the mind when they can't read or spell it, how to find the bus station, how to know where a town is they never heard of before, how to keep in touch with what is left of their kin and keep them from continuing to fall away—how to live.

Novels that are as extravagant and as visionary and yet as fundamentally democratic and simple as *Suttree* restore to American literature a grounding in the humanistic value that the extremes of modernism continue to threaten to dissipate and obscure. For McCarthy a belief in the reality of other people is the first principle of responsible existence, and that is not a theory for him but a vision, complete in itself, expressed not in discourse but in the creation of a world that we are compelled to believe in. Josie Harrogate is the real stroke of genius in this connection. She appears out of nowhere. She is of utterly no consequence to the world at large. She is of no consequence even to this novel's story, which is, after all, over by the time she appears in it. She is a victim of the meanest poverty. She is routinely exposed, as poor people are, both to the steady erosion of health and life and to unpredictable, demeaning violence. This is the story of her life, which, however, she refuses to accept. She has a simple idea of what she must do—and of what, for her, not giving in entails—and she goes on and does it, whether it makes any sense or not. She has kin in McCarthy's other novels as well—those who impose some human rule upon their otherwise bereft lives and change mere living into being.

V The Metaphysics of Violence
Blood Meridian

A little more than two-thirds of the way through *Blood Meridian* is an episode that has the condensed eloquence of a parable. One of the more articulate among the band of Indian-hunters who rule the story, a man referred to as Brown, has come to San Diego to trade for supplies; after an unremembered night of drunken brawling, he seeks out a farrier in town and presents him with a double-barreled shotgun, which he wishes to have sawed down. The gun is English made, with "damascus barrels and engraved locks" and a stock of "burl mahogany."

> There was a raised center rib between the barrels and inlaid in gold the maker's name, London. There were two platinum bands in the patent breech and the locks and the hammers were chased with scrollwork cut deeply in the steel and there were partridges engraved at either end of the maker's name there. The purple barrels were welded up from triple skelps and the hammered iron and steel bore a watered figure like the markings of some alien and antique serpent, rare and beautiful and lethal, and the wood was figured with a deep red feather grain at the butt and held a small springloaded silver capbox in the toe. (pp. 265–66)

The farrier looks from Brown to the gun and back at Brown. "You need what?" he says. "Cut the barrels down," says Brown. "Long about in here. He held a finger across the piece." The farrier refuses to mutilate such an expensive gun and goes so far as to say there must be something wrong with anyone who would. Brown is not pleased, and the moment is tense, for he has killed men for much less reason. Brown offers to pay the man double what he would ordinarily get for the service. The man refuses again and flees to fetch the law. When he returns with a sergeant of the guard, Brown has the gun in the vise and is cutting it down himself. Brown exchanges threatening, caustic words with the sergeant of the guard and then, wholly unperturbed, leaves when he is finished, observing as he goes out that the farrier has disappeared. "I believe that man had done withdrawed his charges," Brown says. "Like as not he was drunk."

What makes this episode worth retelling—as more than a comic anecdote—is the plain truth it speaks as a characterization of not only Brown himself but the entire band of renegades he stands for. The gun has come into Brown's hands as a result of the band's ruthless looting of westward-bound passengers at a ferry crossing. It is more useful to Brown, in his line of work, with short barrels than with long. At the same time, he seems to know instinctively that the gun is a symbol of an order of being, aesthetic and economic, that his whole existence denies. The gun is symbolic in itself, and what Brown does to it is therefore symbolic as well. He knows this, one could say, by not knowing it. The farrier who refuses to butcher the elegant gun is bravely stubborn—braver than he knows—and he has what we would call our better nature on his side. But he cannot handle the matter by himself and has to call in military authority to help him, and he eventually ends by quibbling over not having given Brown permission to use his tools. It finally dawns on him that he is in the presence of something the law itself cannot manipulate, and it is then that he prudently withdraws.

Brown prevails because he is without scruples and because he is oblivious to nuance, to fine ethical discriminations, to social niceties. His authority is a power of nature. He will do anything, and yet what he does to the gun seems right. We imagine the gun's owner, and we find something to respect in Brown's indifference to the ostentatious beauty of the gun and in his lack of the infatuation with craftsmanship that usually turns out to be anxiety about our standing among our peers. He does affect one ornament—an anti-ornament—a scapular of dehydrated human ears, mainly Indian, which he wears to the scaffold when it inevitably comes his turn to die. He inhabits human existence at its geological center, so to speak, where all excrescence, illusion, and philosophical affectation are pared away, leaving a seductively unambiguous core. Needless to say, Brown is not a reflective character, but that is why he is, so to speak, unalienated wherever he is, why he is at home at the center.

One cannot come to terms with McCarthy—and most people won't—without coming to terms with Brown as a representative figure, without determining how it is that in spite of the appalling crudeness and atrocity he is capable of he is also somehow admirable.

Survival as a challenge to manhood is partly what *Blood Meridian* is about. Like his confederates—an ad hoc association of sociopaths—Brown has wholly transcended fear. What we ordinarily refer to as courage is such second nature to him that the term itself seems effete and referentially extraneous. He and the rest live in the presence of death from one day to the next without anxiety and stoically endure excruciating suffering and deprivation. They also live *only* from one day to the next, in a perpetual, moving present. Improvident capitalists, their conglomerate loot the detritus of other people's wealth, they squander all they earn as if not knowing how to take the next step and therefore coercing themselves back to their primal state. They are incapable of maintaining or relating to even the crudest or most venal of social arrangements. They are beyond the pale with a vengeance. McCarthy's other characters from beyond the pale seem like dilettantes by comparison.

Their unpretentious courage, their insouciance, and their resourcefulness as survivors generate a surprising degree of interest and identification. But collectively they also represent a hallowing of the wholly known, the wholly unambiguous. In their opportunistic nihilism they are in a metaphysically safe place: there is no difference for them between what they do and what is. Without revering anything, they are at one with their world. "The only mystery," says Judge Holden, who is the spokesman for this otherwise merely enacted principle, "is that there is no mystery" (p. 252). Their oblivious ferocity indentures them to death, but in a perversely heroic form it also holds mere nothingness at bay. This point is made iconographically when the aimless westward journey ends, as all such journeys do, at the edge of the flattened sea. The mysterious passage that reports this outcome is characteristically rich with the evocation of what life is finally not.

> Loose strands of ambercolored kelp lay in a rubbery wrack at the tideline. A dead seal. Beyond the inner bay part of a reef in a thin line like something foundered there on which the sea was teething. He squatted in the sand and watched the sun on the hammered face of the water. Out there island clouds emplaned upon a salmon colored othersea. Seafowl in silhouette. Downshore the dull surf boomed. There was a horse standing there staring out upon the darkening waters and a young colt that cavorted and trotted off and came back.
> He sat watching while the sun dipped hissing in the swells. The horse stood darkly against the sky. The surf boomed in the dark and the sea's

black hide heaved in the cobbled starlight and the long pale combers loped out of the night and broke along the beach. (pp. 303–304)

As a novel about the American west, *Blood Meridian* presses the psychology of the frontier theory to its logical, appalling extreme. It is not a story for the squeamish, least of all for the philosophically squeamish. But it compels us to call forth from ourselves a capacity for understanding evil that the various meanings of our lives otherwise cause to be suppressed.

To point out that the one articulate spokesman of this novel, Judge Holden, is a direct descendant of Melville's Captain Ahab is to summon up an American tradition—the compulsion to make war upon the unknown, to challenge destiny itself—that helps us make sense of it. To add that he is perhaps even more like Conrad's Kurtz is to fix it in a moral category that deals with the psychopathology of conquest. If Marlow were in this novel rather than his own, he would still surely say at some point, as a bridge between us and the outer limit:

> Ugly. Yes it was ugly enough; but if you were man enough you would admit to yourself that there was in you just the faintest trace of a response to the terrible frankness of that noise, a dim suspicion of there being a meaning in it which you—you so remote from the night of the first ages— could comprehend. And why not? The mind of man is capable of anything—because everything is in it, all the past as well as all the future.

Reading back to *Heart of Darkness* from *Blood Meridian* reminds us that Marlow's confession is tinged with regret as well as self-reassuring relief, since obviously Kurtz would not be worth telling stories about if he were not, so to speak, one of us. Since no Marlow exists in *Blood Meridian*, we are there in Marlow's place. In fact, Judge Holden is such an imposing conception and such a bizarre intellectual, as well as physical, presence partly because he is both Marlow and Kurtz; and he is a more terrifying figure than either Ahab or Kurtz because his madness is wholly under control and because he rather than justice—divine or social—prevails. It is the man of scruples—however minimal—who is the judge's true adversary and who, because of his scruples and his unwillingness not to be judged, eventually dies. This man is merely a boy when the bloody action begins, called only "the kid." When he and the judge face each other as last survivors in the desert, the judge calls out to him: "There's a flawed place in the fabric of your heart. Do you think I could not know? You alone were mutinous. You alone reserved in your soul some corner of clemency for the heathen" (p. 299).

When they next encounter each other, the kid in jail, the judge declares that the kid had failed the common good by being a witness against himself. "You sat in judgement on your own deeds. You put your own allowances before the judgements of history and you broke with the body of which you even pledged a part. . . . [Each] was called upon to empty out his heart into the common and one did not" (p. 307). The judge refers to no action of the kid's, no betrayal, for no one of this band he alludes to has been less murderous than another. He has merely surmised that the kid has harbored a scruple in his heart, and by the perverse logic that rules the judge's system of values, even this modest breach of faith is impermissible. The confirming sign of it is the kid's inability to kill the judge and his leashed, attending fool when he has them in his sights. The judge has turned ordinary moral law on its head. "War is God," he proclaims (p. 249), and this odd shibboleth is supported in the novel by a genuine metaphysic that piece by piece the judge articulates. It is enacted everywhere in the novel by his dimmer protégés. It is put into words, with a Jacobean grandeur and cogency, only by the judge.

To put the theory before the fact—which reverses the priority of the narrative—this is how it goes. The judge is a worshiper of truth. Truth is what can be known, not what can be supposed or dreamed up. He therefore absolutizes history because history is the repository of all that can be known. History is all that can prove anything.

> A moral view can never be proven right or wrong by any ultimate test. A man falling dead in a duel is not thought thereby to be proven in error as to his views. His very involvement in such a trial gives evidence of a new and broader view. The willingness of the principals to forgo further argument as the triviality which it in fact is and to petition directly the chambers of the historical absolute clearly indicates of how little moment are the opinions and of what great moment the divergences thereof. For the argument is indeed trivial, but not so the separate wills thereby made manifest. (p. 250)

Certitude and will are all that matter, the one dependent upon the other. "Moral law is an invention of mankind for the disenfranchisement of the powerful in favor of the weak. Historical law subverts it at every turn." (The judge is an older contemporary of Nietzsche's and can't very well have read him.) The infallibility of this doctrine, not the moral coarseness that it validates only as a corollary, is the basis of its appeal.

> Man's vanity may well approach the infinite in capacity but his knowledge remains imperfect and howevermuch he comes to value his judgements ultimately he must submit them before a higher court. Here there can be no special pleading. Here are considerations of equity and rectitude and moral right rendered void and without warrant and here are the views of the litigants despised. Decisions of life and death, of what shall be and what shall not, beggar all questions of right. In elections of these magnitudes are all lesser ones subsumed, moral, spiritual, natural. (p. 250)

The man who here proclaims that war is God is affirming a rigorous metaphysic, not claiming an excuse for barbarism. The empirical premise of his argument is a sadly persuasive one. "If war is not holy man is nothing but antic clay."

Some other metaphysic would conceivably be preferable, some other system in which to believe and from which to infer and assign value. But man—and the gender term is appropriate here—has produced firm evidence in history that only violence recurs as the indisputable common denominator of his presence in time. War therefore must be holy, or must be affirmed as being holy, for man's existence to have any sanctity at all, for war is the main feature of human experience. There is a certain unpleasant logic to this reasoning and an element of pathos as well, since it is testimony—and meant to be testimony—to the paucity of any other evidence of the sanctity of human existence.

Judge Holden might be regarded as a failed priest, and he in fact is shadowed by an ex-priest, of whom the judge says (for the ex-priest is one of the band of Indian-slayers): "the priest has put by the robes of his craft and taken up the tools of that higher calling which all men honor" (p. 250). And it is the judge who perceives that their conditions as students of metaphysics are analogous: "Men of god and men of war have strange affinities." But the only rituals that are true rituals, he says at the end, are those that entail the shedding of blood. All others are mock rituals, empty abstractions, ceremonies of progressively lesser degree.

> Here every man knows the false at once. Never doubt it. That feeling in the breast that evokes a child's memory of loneliness such as when the others have gone and only the game is left with its solitary participant. A solitary game, without opponent. Where only the rules are at hazard. Dont

look away. We are not speaking in mysteries. You of all men are no stranger to that feeling, the emptiness and the despair. It is that which we take arms against, is it not? (p. 329)

The emptiness and the despair: the judge's false religion originates in the same existential vacuum as any other; and given the distortions that logic can thrive upon, it is as rational as any other. "[Each] man's destiny is as large as the world he inhabits and contains within it all opposites as well. This desert upon which so many have been broken is vast and calls for largeness of heart but it is also ultimately empty. It is hard, it is barren. Its very nature is stone" (p. 230). The judge's obsession is simple. He wishes to take command of that empty space—empty of value, empty of meaning—and fill it with his own presence. "Whatever in creation exists without my knowledge exists without my consent.... Only nature can enslave man and only when the existence of each last entity is routed out and made to stand naked before him will he be properly suzerain of the earth" (p. 198).

> The man who believes that the secrets of the world are forever hidden lives in mystery and fear. Superstition will drag him down. The rain will erode the deeds of his life. But that man who sets himself the task of singling out the thread of order from the tapestry will by the decision alone have taken charge of the world and it is only by such taking charge that he will effect a way to dictate the terms of his own fate. (pp. 198–99)

If the judge is a failed priest, he may as well be Satan; but if he is Satan, he may as well be God also, for in this context the two are not conceived as inversions of one another. The arguments on behalf of one turn out to be the same as those for the other, and in that paradox lies the appalling moral of the judge's story. We are compelled by it to envision a *tertium quid*, but the evidence of some other thread of order in this tapestry is not easy to discover.

The challenge is made doubly difficult not only because the judge prevails at the end and because he has no serious philosophical adversary in the text but also because the mercenaries, for whom he is the unappointed spokesman, repeatedly prove his case, in their actions if not in their words. They reject the implications of his argument. "The good book says that he that lives by the sword shall perish by the sword," says the black man named Jackson, who has recently beheaded his white confederate, also named Jackson. "That's some more of your craziness," says Brown, who wears the necklace of Indian ears. "Might does not make right," says Irving, no less vicious than the rest. "The man that wins in some combat is not vindicated morally" (p. 250). On one occasion, as the mercenaries leave behind at night a doomed band of prospectors, they each seem visited by a forlorn nostalgia. One of the dying prospectors they can hear singing as they ride away. The man is alternately singing hymns to and cursing God. "[They] could hear the hymns of their childhood and they could hear them as they ascended the arroyo and rode up through the low junipers wet with rain. The dying man sang with great clarity and intention and the riders setting forth upcountry may have ridden more slowly the longer to hear him for they were of just these qualities themselves" (p. 119).

Such unironic sentimentality on their part is not clearheaded by the judge's standard. Their feeling is merely vestigial, as discontinuous with the facts of their lives and their behavior as their words are: "The man that wins in some combat is not vindicated morally," for instance. (The judge is different from his surly companions only in being wholly at one with himself, beyond scruples.) Otherwise they kill and rape and pillage without restraint and on a scale that staggers the imagination and repeatedly affronts the eye with gory spectacle. Mere greed could not account for such slaughter; the stakes are clearly much higher. The motives are darker and more irrational than greed. The men wish to distance themselves from the judge's pretentious rhetoric, but they prove his case in their deeds, and the judge's words in relation to their actions are like the chased scrollwork or the platinum bands or the feathered grain of the stock of the shotgun that Brown has cut down to size, to the matter of fact. With their lives they have made a ceremony of survival—as the judge well knows.

> Men are born for games. Nothing else. Every child knows that play is nobler than work. He knows too that the worth or merit of a game is not inherent in the game itself but rather in the value of that which is put at hazard.... Suppose two men at cards with nothing to wager save their lives. Who has not heard such a tale? A turn of the card. The whole universe for such a player has labored clanking to this moment which will tell if he is to die at that man's hand or that man at his. What more certain validation of a man's worth could there be? (p. 249)

It is a nice, unliberal irony of McCarthy's story that the Indians in it are if anything more deranged and barbarous than the white men and more surrealistically discontinuous from any known patterns of human behavior. What their own Judge Holden might say about their motives is beyond our comprehension.

> They halted and sat their horses. The party approaching were clad in such fool's regalia and withal bore themselves with such aplomb that the paler riders were hard put to keep their composure. The leader was a man named Caballo en Pelo and this old mogul wore a belted wool overcoat that would have served a far colder climate and beneath it a woman's blouse of embroidered silk and a pair of pantaloons of gray cassinette. He was small and wiry and he had lost an eye to the Maricopas and he presented the Americans with a strange priapic leer that may have at one time been a smile. At his right rode a lesser chieftain named Pascual in a frogged coat out at the elbows and who wore in his nose a bone hung with small pendants. The third man was Pablo and he was clad in a scarlet coat with tarnished braiding and tarnished epaulettes of silver wire. He was barefooted and bare of leg and he wore on his face a pair of round green goggles. In this attire they arranged themselves before the Americans and nodded austerely. (pp. 254–55)

They are wonders of the imagination, and yet we have the queasy feeling that we are being told, for the first time, the raw, unromantic truth about both sides in the war for the Southwest territories. To a remarkable degree the evil of suffering, which in *Suttree* merely impinged upon human life, in *Blood Meridian* has metastasized and become human. The difference is extraordinary. Like *The Orchard Keeper* and *Outer Dark*, the two novels make a fit by being dialectical inversions of each other.

This contrast is especially vivid when *Blood Meridian* is read as a critique of our culture's anthropocentrism. What the judge says and he and his confederates act out eventually seems like an only slightly demented revival of Enlightenment philosophy, and the judge's intellectual imperialism may be read finally as an instance of what happens if Enlightenment doctrine is pressed to its logical conclusion. The judge is a naturalist as well as a warrior-intellectual. He carries a journal with him, Darwinlike, in which he records the curious patterns of stones, insects, fossils, plants. He shoots the rare birds of new terrains, stuffs them with dried grass, and keeps them as specimens. He collects the leaves of unusual bushes and trees. He catches exotic butterflies with his shirt. It is when he is entering a set of observations in his journal that he says to a dubious witness, "Whatever in creation exists without my knowledge exists without my consent"; and when the witness argues plausibly that no man can acquaint himself with everything on this earth, the judge simply paraphases the time-honored faith of the *philosophes*: "The man who believes

THE METAPHYSICS OF VIOLENCE   125

that the secrets of the world are forever hidden lives in mystery and fear. Superstition will drag him down. The rain will erode the deeds of his life" (p. 199). His true and unspoken motivation is illustrated when one day at a natural cistern near El Paso he reproduces in his notebook ancient Indian wall paintings of men, animals, birds, arcane maps, and bright abstract designs—and then, having so taken possession of them, chooses one of the designs to stand for the whole and symbolically scrapes it away, "leaving no trace of it only a raw place on the stone where it had been" (p. 173).

As he says later, everything in his view is predicated on there being "no mystery," but again in these moments he seems to be saying more than he intends. He seems in fact to fear that there is indeed a mystery and that its being would deny his own. The very coherence of his argument and the cold passion of his commitment to it intimate a psychic rigidity born of dread. In a sense, it is his own passion for a clearheaded logical confrontation of issues that he has to fear most. For having argued that "the only mystery is that there is no mystery," he later finds himself arguing, in effect, the reverse:

> The truth about the world, he said, is that anything is possible. Had you not seen it all from birth and thereby bled it of its strangeness it would appear to you for what it is, a hat trick in a medicine show, a fevered dream, a trance bepopulate with chimeras having neither analogue nor precedent, an itinerant carnival, a migratory tentshow whose ultimate destination after many a pitch in many a mudded field is unspeakable and calamitous beyond reckoning.
>
> The universe is no narrow thing and the order within it is not constrained by any latitude in its conception to repeat what exists in one part in any other part. Even in this world more things exist without our knowledge than with it and the order in creation which you see is that which you have put there, like a string in a maze, so that you shall not lose your way. For existence has its own order and that no man's mind can compass that mind itself being but a fact among others. (p. 245)

This argument makes him seem to have been transformed before our eyes from Voltaire into Kant and then into Heidegger. The contradictions are apparent, though for the judge and his slow-witted pupils the authority of his presence and conviction compels all such incompatible distinctions to seem as one. The fact that his rhetorical authority obscures real contradictions for both himself and his listeners is a sign that he has contrived a belief system for which unwavering conviction itself is the objective.

It is the very cornerstone of his own argument that the judge himself discloses to be fundamentally insecure. Having appealed to the evidence of "historical law," to the "historical absolute," to support his claim that war and power are sacred, he subsequently attempts to argue—toward another end—that the reality of the past can be subject to doubt because the power of the human mind that seeks to recall it is fallible.

> The straight and the winding way are one and now that you are here what do the years count since last we two met together? Men's memories are uncertain and the past that was differs little from the past that was not.
> He took up the tumbler the judge had poured and he drank and set it down again. He looked at the judge. I been everwhere, he said. This is just one more place.
> The judge arched his brow. Did you post witnesses? he said. To report to you on the continuing existence of those places once you'd quit them?
> That's crazy.
> Is it? Where is yesterday? Where is Glanton and Brown and where is the priest? He leaned closer. Where is Shelby, whom you left to the mercies of Elias in the desert, and where is Tate whom you abandoned in the mountains? Where are the ladies, ah the fair and tender ladies with whom you danced at the governor's ball when you were a hero anointed with the blood of the enemies of the republic you'd elected to defend? And where is the fiddler and where the dance? (pp. 330–31)

This passage can be read to argue that the mind is fallible, that memory is irrelevant, or that the present in consciousness is all; but any way it is read, it does not substantiate an appeal to the absoluteness of history. The consistency on one point that produces the inconsistency on the other is, of course, Judge Holden's obsessive fidelity only to what is known, to what is in the foreground of consciousness. Like another famous American egotist, Isabel Archer, he has trouble summoning the reality of absent people. He cannot be concerned with the implications of his own observation that "in this world more things exist without our knowledge than with it." His extreme of logic, as Wallace Stevens said of another ideologue, is illogical.

In an earlier part of the narrative, before the judge had taken command of it, this whole thematic pattern had been set in context for us by a random philosophical exchange between the barely articulate "kid" and an old hermit he has come across in the prairie.

> The old man swung his head back and forth. The way of the transgressor is hard. God made this world, but he didnt make it to suit everybody, did he?

> I dont believe he much had me in mind.
> Aye, said the old man. But where does a man come by his notions. What world's he seen that he liked better?
> I can think of better places and better ways.
> Can ye make it be?
> No.
> No. It's a mystery. A man's at odds to know his mind cause his mind is aught he has to know it with. He can know his heart, but he dont want to. Rightly so. Best not to look in there. It aint the heart of a creature that is bound in the way that God has set for it. You can find meanness in the least of creatures, but when God made man the devil was at his elbow. A creature that can do anything. Make a machine. And a machine to make the machine. And evil that can run itself a thousand years, no need to tend it. You believe that?
> I dont know.
> Believe that. (p. 19)

McCarthy's own rhetorical strategy repeatedly emphasizes the elusive nature of the truth. The old hermit's words seem to us sound, and we certainly see his point about evil in the ensuing 318 pages of text. His eloquently expressed judgment of the limits of self-knowledge foreshadows the judge's description of the mind as a fact among others. He comes closer to speaking the paraphrased theme of the novel than any other spokesman. Yet he himself is admittedly a former slave hunter; he carries the dried heart of a black man he has killed; and he believes, he says, that the four things that will destroy the earth are "women, whiskey, money, and niggers" (p. 18). His own nature proves the point of his observations about human nature in general. The book itself makes his point more persuasively, and the *whole* point includes the crucial but recessive one that a better world *can* be imagined, though the source of such a notion is obscure and the making it real is impossible.

> Aye, said the old man. But where does a man come by his notions. What world's he seen that he liked better?
> I can think of better places and better ways.
> Can you make it be?
> No.
> No. It's a mystery. (p. 19)

It is a mystery, indeed, but the mystery—as usual in McCarthy's work—is the mystery as much of art as of human nature, for the other truth of this story lives in words and apart from the action, from character, from the judge's rhetoric, from the ordinary and sense-making facility of the mind. Insofar as it is real only in language, it is a human reality. But insofar as this language is a mediation, it is of the world as well, though what it may be said to mean in conventional discourse is beyond claiming. *Blood Meridian* is haunted by the mystery that its own language challenges the very nihilistic logic that it gives representation to. The language itself is a presence, and the world as it enters into language is a presence; and whatever it is that this presence may be said to be is precisely what the judge and his cerebral violence have declared war upon. The richness generated out of such morally impoverished material seems intended to appear miraculous and in some sense transcendent and beyond the reach of the mind, which is finally merely a fact among others. McCarthy is closer to Hemingway than to Faulkner in this respect. The work of such an idiom shows itself most clearly in a reverence for nature and for the way in which nature corresponds to an imagined condition of being that the facts of life otherwise contradict.

> All that day they climbed through a highland part forested with joshua trees and rimmed about by bald granite peaks. In the evening flocks of eagles went up through the pass before them and they could see on those grassy benches the great shambling figures of bears like cattle grazing on some upland heath. There were skifts of snow in the lee of the stone ledges and in the night a light snow fell upon them. Reefs of mist were blowing across the slopes when they set out shivering in the dawn and in the new snow they saw the tracks of the bears that had come down to take their wind just before daylight.
> That day there was no sun only a paleness in the haze and the country was white with frost and shrubs were like polar isomers of their own shapes. Wild rams ghosted away up those rocky draws and the wind swirled down cold and gray from the snowy reeks above them, a smoking region of wild vapors blowing down through the gap as if the world up there were all afire. They spoke less and less between them until at last they were silent altogether as is often the way with travelers approaching the end of a journey. (pp. 302–303)
>
> They descended by rocky switchbacks and across the beds of streams where small trout stood on their pale fins and studied the noses of the drinking horses. Sheets of mist that smelled and tasted of metal rose out of the gorge and crossed over them and moved on through the woods. They nudged the horses through the ford and down the trace and at three oclock in the afternoon in a thin and drizzling rain they rode into the old stone town of Jesus Maria. (p. 188)
>
> They rode up switchbacks through a lonely aspen wood where the fallen leaves lay like golden disclets in the damp black trail. The leaves shifted in

a million spangles down the pale corridors and Glanton took one and turned it like a tiny fan by its stem and held it and let it fall and its perfection was not lost on him. They rode through a narrow draw where the leaves were shingled up in ice and they crossed a high saddle at sunset where wild doves were rocketing down the wind and passing through the gap a few feet off the ground, veering wildly among the ponies and dropping off down into the blue gulf below. (p. 136)

Whether because of changing light or the dwarfing effect of massive landscapes, or because of our being seen from another world, or because of creatures taking flight into a space outside the frame, our perspective is never stable in the way the judge insists it must be. Nor are the sweetness of mist and of new snow or the dignity of eagles or the elegance of stationary trout in a clear stream—all such things so incongruous against the backdrop of gore and human depravity—the only signs of a world within our world. That would be more facile and Wordsworthian than McCarthy is capable of being. The not-human world in this novel seems to be competing on every page in every natural detail for a standing equivalent to the human.

> In the neuter austerity of that terrain all phenomena were bequeathed a strange equality and no one thing nor spider nor stone nor blade of grass could put forth claim to precedence. The very clarity of these articles belied their familiarity, for the eye predicates the whole on some feature or part and here was nothing more luminous than another and nothing more enshadowed and in the optical democracy of such landscapes all preference is made whimsical and a man and a rock become endowed with unguessed kinships. (p. 247)

Such unguessed kinships in a democracy that is more than merely optical are very much to the point of *Blood Meridian*'s baroque density, and our assumptions about the place of human power over the world are thereby called into question. This was Hemingway's way of being religious without believing, and it is McCarthy's as well. But McCarthy's vision is more complex because the indwelling reality that his language evokes lies as mysteriously and as vividly in the grotesque as in the conventionally beautiful; because it is not simple-minded, it is more persuasive. Here, of course, language is all. Without the extraordinary ear and photorealistic eye and command of metaphor that are McCarthy's unique gift, the effect of verbal apotheosis would remain insipid and inert. But language transforms the world of *Blood Meridian* into a magic kingdom, and what lives there can only be said to defy logic.

That night they rode through a region electric and wild where strange shapes of soft blue bire ran over the metal of the horses' trappings and the wagonwheels rolled in hoops of fire and little shapes of pale blue light came to perch in the ears of the horses and the beards of the men. All night sheetlightning quaked sourceless to the west beyond the midnight thunderheads, making a bluish day of the distant desert, the mountains on the sudden skyline stark and black and livid like a land of some other order out there whose true geology was not stone but fear. The thunder moved up from the southwest and lightning lit the desert all about them, blue and barren, great clanging reaches ordered out of the absolute night like some demon kingdom summoned up or changeling land that come the day would leave them neither trace nor smoke nor ruin more than any troubling dream. (p. 47)

This ferry was taken over by the Yumas and operated for them by a man named Callaghan, but within days it was burned and Callaghan's headless body floated anonymously downriver, a vulture standing between the shoulderblades in clerical black, silent rider to the sea. (p. 262)

The savages built a bonfire on the hill and fueled it with the furnishings from the white men's quarters and they raised up Glanton's body and bore it aloft in the manner of a slain champion and hurled it onto the flames. They'd tied his dog to his corpse and it was snatched after in howling suttee to disappear crackling in the rolling greenwood smoke. The doctor's torso was dragged up by the heels and raised and flung onto the pyre and the doctor's mastiff also was committed to the flames. It slid struggling down the far side and the thongs with which it was tied must have burnt in two for it began to crawl charred and blind and smoking from the fire and was flung back with a shovel. The other bodies eight in number were heaped onto the fire where they sizzled and stank and the thick smoke rolled out over the river. The doctor's head had been mounted upon a paling and carried about but at the last it too was thrown onto the blaze. The guns and clothing were divided upon the clay and divided too were the gold and silver out of the hacked and splintered chest that they'd dragged forth. All else was heaped on the flames and while the sun rose and glistened on their gaudy faces they sat upon the ground each with his new goods before him and they watched the fire and smoked their pipes as might some painted troupe of mimefolk recruiting themselves in such a wayplace far from the towns and the rabble hooting at them across the smoking footlamps, contemplating towns to come and the poor fanfare of trumpet and drum and the rude boards upon which their destinies were inscribed for these people were no less bound and indentured and they watched like the prefiguration of their own ends the carbonized skulls of their enemies incandescing before them bright as blood among the coals. (pp. 275–76)

Saddletrees eaten bare of their rawhide coverings and weathered white as bone, a light chamfering of miceteeth along the edges of the wood. They rode through a region where iron will not rust nor tin tarnish. The ribbed frames of dead cattle under their patches of dried hide lay like the ruins of primitive boats upturned upon that shoreless void and they passed lurid and austere the black and desiccated shapes of horses and mules that travelers had stood afoot. These parched beasts had died with their necks stretched in agony in the sand and now upright and blind and lurching askew with scraps of blackened leather hanging from the fretwork of their ribs leaned with their long mouths howling after the endless tandem suns that passed above them. (pp. 246–47)

They went on, the kid with his pistol drawn, stepping and ducking the shafts where they fell out of the sun, the lengths of them glistening against the pale sky and foreshortening in a reedy flutter and then suddenly quivering dead in the ground. They snapped off the shafts against their being used again and they labored on sideways over the sand like crabs until the arrows coming so thick and close they made a stand. . . . They were twenty-four hours without water and the barren mural of sand and sky was beginning to shimmer and swim and the periodic arrows sprang aslant from the sands about them like the tufted stalks of mutant desert growths propagating angrily into the dry desert air. (pp. 278–79)

It was a lone tree burning on the desert. A heraldic tree that the passing storm had left afire. The solitary pilgrim drawn up before it had traveled far to be here and he knelt in the hot sand and held his numbed hands out while all about in that circle attended companies of lesser auxiliaries routed forth into the inordinate day, small owls that crouched silently and stood from foot to foot and tarantulas and solpugas and vinegarroons and the vicious mygale spiders and beaded lizards with mouths black as chowdog's, deadly to man, and the little desert basilisks that jet blood from their eyes and the small sandvipers like seemly gods, silent and the same, in Jeda, in Babylon. A constellation of ignited eyes that edged the ring of light all bound in a precarious truce before this torch whose brightness had set back the stars in their sockets. (p. 215)

The material world in *Blood Meridian*, even in death and desolation, seems always to become in the mediated form of McCarthy's language more than itself, not only exotic but transubstantiated. That action in the style is like a separate story going on. As with the arrows propagating like desert plants or the bones of cattle in the desert becoming the ribs of beached sea vesels, some other unknowable kind of will seems at work in this world that is oblivious to the will of men. The effect is reinforced by the very nature of simile, which simultaneously clarifies what is before us and draws our attention off into a different space. When similes proliferate as they do in *Blood Meridian*, crowding in upon one another or rhythmically recurring, the role of the double image that simile presents begins to take on significance in itself:

> He looked at the expriest and at the slow gouts of blood dropping in the water like roseblooms how they swelled and were made pale. (p. 291)
>
> Then he saw the idiot shambling along behind them like some dim neolithic herdsman. (p. 288)
>
> He struck out across the barren pan, nothing but sparse tufts of grass and the widely scattered palmilla standing solitary and silent against the lowering sky like other beings posted there. (p. 214)
>
> That night they were visitwith a plague of hail out of a faultless sky and the horses shied and moaned and the men dismounted and sat upon the ground with their saddles over their heads while the hail leaped in the sand like small lucent eggs concocted alchemically out of the desert darkness. When they resaddled and rode on they went for miles through cobbled ice while a polar moon rose like a blind cat's eye up over the rim of the world. In the night they passed the lights of a village on the plain but they did not alter from their course. (p. 152)
>
> All to the north the rain had dragged black tendrils down from the thunderclouds like tracings of lampblack fallen in a beaker and in the night they could hear the drum of rain miles away on the prairie. (p. 186)
>
> They climbed up through rolling grasslands where small birds shied away chittering down the wind and a buzzard labored up from among bones with wings that went whoop whoop whoop like a child's toy swung on a string and in the long red sunset the sheets of water on the plain below them lay like tidepools of primal blood. (p. 187)

There are many such wonders as the burning tree for men and creatures—momentarily like "seemly gods"—to gaze upon with dignity. What with any other novelist would be a merely ornate style repeatedly seems to move us toward an epiphany, though only the kind that a seasoned gnostic might construe. And though certainly the brutish human will, in its articulate and inarticulate forms, prevails and rules over the other narrative, the nature of being human in the overall text is finally ambiguous. The human body, Blake's "human form divine," cannot easily be thought of again as a coherent form of any kind, let alone as the temple of the holy spirit: dead babies hung by their underjaws from the limbs of bushes to stare sightless at the sky; double handfuls of brains blown out of the backs of skulls; a man's head cut off to roll into the campfire while the columns of blood from his neck subside to bubble gently like a stew; men hung upside down, above a fire, skewered through their heels, until their brains cook and steam sings from their nostrils. After such nightmarish dismemberment and evisceration and decay, what is precious to us may seem immeasurably more precious for being defiled; and yet it seems grotesquely negligible as well. This is a leveling effect as well as a horrifying one, a democratizing of species, an enhancement of the being of the world and a relegation of the human.

The landscape lends a panoramic grandeur to the spectacles of conflict, bloodlettings, and stoic endurance and causes the otherwise meaningless procession westward to seem like a dream of history. And yet it also diminishes the events and the human participants in them. The farthest reach of this landscape is the stars, so the distance of the constellations in their void, their impersonal autonomy, becomes a sobering theme in itself. One expression of it forms a nicely appropriate parable about the relationship between nature and the human will. One night, when the kid and the ex-priest are trying to make progress across the desert in the darkness, they fall asleep and wake to find that the very constellations they had navigated by have disappeared.

The thought that is difficult to hold in focus is that nature in *Blood Meridian*, as in all of McCarthy's novels, is both a void and an emanation. In either role it is not analogous to the categories of thought. If we think of the whole of *Blood Meridian* as a parable, it is a perfect vehicle for representing the futility of the human will—because of, not despite, the hubris that the Indian-killers embody and the judge rationalizes. The human beings constitute one protagonist and the natural world another. Narrative and description collaborate with each other in conventional ways, but what is ultimately important is that, even ontologically, they compete.

Pondering the implications of *Blood Meridian* and the way it is written, the way in which the rich style and the impoverished subject matter interact with each other, brings to mind words that Henry James once wrote to H. G. Wells on the subject of how art and reality are mutually dependent: "It is art that *makes* life, makes interest, makes importance, for our consideration and application of those things, and I know of no substitute whatever for the force and beauty of the process." This purpose, by which the artist claims the role of a withdrawn God and by which, accomplished, the world becomes as it should have been, may be the only claim the maker of *Blood Meridian* would be bold enough to make.

An alternate view from within the novel and obliquely supported by it is the homily spoken by the ex-priest, Tobin.

> Oh it may be the Lord's way of showin how little store he sets by the learned. Whatever could it mean to one who knows all? He's an uncommon love for the common man and godly wisdom resides in the least of things so that it may well be that the voice of the Almighty speaks most profoundly in such beings as lives in silence themselves.
>
> He watched the kid.
>
> For let it go how it will, he said, God speaks in the least of creatures.
>
> The kid thought him to mean birds or things that crawl but the expriest, watching, his head slightly cocked, said: No man is give leave of that voice.
>
> The kid spat into the fire and bent to his work.
>
> I aint heard no voice, he said.
>
> When it stops, said Tobin, you'll know you've heard it all your life.
>
> Is that right?
>
> Aye.
>
> The kid turned the leather in his lap. The expriest watched him.
>
> At night, said Tobin, when the horses are grazing and the company is asleep, who hears them grazing?
>
> Dont nobody hear them if they're asleep.
>
> Aye. And if they cease their grazing who is it that wakes?
>
> Every man.
>
> Aye, said the expriest. Every man. (pp. 123-24)

But it may also be that in *Blood Meridian* human evil, as Judge Holden would have it, has taken an irreversible form. For as this judge prevails, the sworn enemy of unreason and the ideological murderer of innocents—of a Mexican boy, of an Indian girl, of a mere puppy, and of the kid who has betrayed by his scruple—he also dances. "Only that man who has offered up himself entire to the blood of war, who has been to the floor of the pit and seen horror in the round and learned at last that it speaks to its inmost heart, only that man can dance" (p. 331). Thus our version here of looking off into the heart of an imminent darkness is a small apocalypse, a primitive ceremony in which life and death have been forced to become one.

> And they are dancing, the board floor slamming under the jackboots and the fiddlers grinning hideously over their canted pieces. Towering over them all is the judge and he is naked dancing, his small feet lively and

quick and now in doubletime and bowing to the ladies, huge and pale and hairless, like an enormous infant. He never sleeps, he says. He says he'll never die. He bows to the fiddlers and sashays backwards and throws back his head and laughs deep in his throat and he is a great favorite, the judge. He wafts his hat and the lunar dome of his skull passes palely under the lamps and he swings about and takes possession of one of the fiddles and he pirouettes and makes a pass, two passes, dancing and fiddling at once. His feet are light and nimble. He never sleeps. He says that he will never die. He dances in light and in shadow and he is a great favorite. He never sleeps, the judge. He is dancing, dancing. He says that he will never die. (p. 335)

When Judge Holden and what he embodies prevail in history everything that is otherwise allowed to flourish in language and its mediation of nature and the world, what is not known and not knowable, must become extinct. The judge and the idiot child that he keeps throughout the last half of the novel as a human mascot are fit companions, for each is the ultimate extension of the other, each alienated—one by will, the other by the absence of it—from the ambiguous and marginal conditions of being that waver before thought.

Such overlapping readings of *Blood Meridian* recall similar problems with *Suttree* and remind us of Suttree's returning to the scenes of his Catholic childhood, only to be disillusioned over and over again, of his forlorn desire to recover a sacred value from the detritus of human aspiration. This intransitive desire of Suttree's suggests that the ex-priest's words about God speaking in silence have more weight than their comparatively relegated position in the novel would seem to cause them to have. However, the whole experience of McCarthy's work—as one novel clashes with another—is that nothing can be taken to stand as the truth. Anything that *stands* in this sense by definition cannot be true. For in such novels truth is not an imaginable but inaccessible form—what remains stable apart from the flux of our experience; nor is it the product of a dialectic. Truth is the dialectic itself, an unending contest between the stubbornness of fact and the irrepressibility of desire.

Bibliography

Bell, Vereen M. "The Ambiguous Nihilism of Cormac McCarthy." *Southern Literary Journal*, XV (Spring, 1983), 31–41.

Broyard, Anatole. "Daddy Quit, She Said." In *Aroused by Books*. New York, 1974.

In *Child of God*, McCarthy "has [the] best kind of Southern style, fusing risky eloquence, intricate rhythms and dead-to-rights accuracy." ("I've often wondered whether this kind of writing—William Faulkner is the classical example—isn't partly the result of the black influence on Southern speech, a stress on sonorousness and musicality.") McCarthy "doesn't fall into the familiar error of forcing all of his people to talk 'poetically' simply because they live in the rural south." Lester Ballard, for example, "knows talking won't help him and he doesn't fool with it. His silence is in tense counterpoint to the tumult of his actions." There aren't "many authors who know how to use silence or terseness, who can strip a character's speech down to bare necessity so that his whole personality becomes a kind of aposiopesis, a breaking off for dramatic effect." Lester's clothing the dead girl and then going outside to look at her through the window is a kind of perverted poetry. McCarthy shows how a good writer can make us care about a "bad" character.

———. "Where All Tales Are Tall." *New York Times*, January 20, 1979, p. 19.

In *Suttree*, McCarthy's writing is "a hypnosis of detail." "He makes you feel that, because this place is palpably real, these events would seem to be true. His people are so vivid they seem exotic, but this is just another way of saying that we tend to forget the range of human differences." "McCarthy's hyperbole is not Southern rhetoric, but flesh and blood. Every tale is tall, if you look at it closely enough." "Yes, there are a lot of dead people in *Suttree* but then people do die, especially poor and stubborn and violent ones. And Southerners, including Southern writers, don't believe in abandoning their dead."

Coles, Robert. "The Stranger." *New Yorker*, August 26, 1974, pp. 87–90.

In *Child of God*, McCarthy "seems not to wish our 20th century psychological sensibility to influence his work." Ballard's "state of mind [is] not the subject of inquiry." McCarthy is a "strange incompatible" mixture of ancient Greek dramatist and medieval moralist: his characters seem at the same time blind to self and driven by forces outside control—desperately wayward ones who will be judged by God. McCarthy's novels tell us we cannot understand human idiosyncrasy—why some men are haunted Ballards and some live easily with kin and neighbors. McCarthy is a novelist "of religious feeling": "His characters are by explicit designation children of whoever or whatever it is that we fall back upon when we want to evoke the vastness or mystery of this universe, and our comparative ignorance and uncertainty." McCarthy's "mordant wit and refusal to bend to literary and intellectual demands of our era" will leave him unknown and misinterpreted.

Davenport, Guy. "Appalachian Gothic." *New York Times Book Review*, September 29, 1968, Sec. 7, p. 4.

In *Outer Dark*, Appalachian speechways are "timeless epic diction." McCarthy is "unashamedly an allegorist" with a belief in the "absolute destructiveness" of evil. The theme here is "lucklessness"; the plot unfolds like Greek tragedy with logical inevitability. The theme and locale are "impressively ancient"—what is original is the *style*: "Appalachian phrases as plain and as functional as an ax" and the "elegant counter point" of bookish diction. McCarthy "doesn't waste a word" on characters' thoughts; with total objectivity he describes what they do and records their speech.

———. "Silurian Southern." *National Review*, March 16, 1979, pp. 368–69.

In *Suttree*, McCarthy's characters do not "think": McCarthy has "subtracted from narrative tradition that running account . . . of rationalization, opinion and intent." "Critics have sniped at McCarthy's studied prose rhythms and unfamiliar words not seeing the need he has of them." "He must summon his world before our eyes, in all its richness and exactness of shape, because that is all he is summoning." What fascinates McCarthy is the "irrational intrepidity" of people. He has a radically original way with tone—a sense of the aloneness of people in their individuality. Suttree as character allows the author for the first time a limited amount of interiority—a character who might be a projection of the author—making Suttree a protagonist with a "subjective cast."

Ditsky, John. "Further into Darkness: The Novels of Cormac McCarthy." *Hollins Critic*, XVIII (April, 1981), 1–11.

McCarthy is in diction and tone "beyond Faulkner"—"as if there were no limits to what language might be pushed into doing in the last half of the twentieth century." The clash between his "near-incredible erudition and resources of diction and actual subject matter" creates "enormous and disturbing energy." In *Outer Dark*, events "occur generally in a void—they rivet attention because they are all that exists, and they take precisely the time it takes to read of them to happen." *Child of God* combines "elaborate diction" with "terrible deeds"—creating a tension of "attraction" and "repulsion." This is not comic-strip violence, then, but more akin to Yeats's "terrible beauty." The protagonist in *Suttree* has gifts for coping that none of McCarthy's other characters have—he is almost a stereotypical sixties dropout: articulate and intelligent. McCarthy's style combines a "regional ear" with a "poet's sense of rhythm."

Schaefer, William J. "Cormac McCarthy: The Hard Wages of Original Sin." *Appalachian Journal*, IV (1976–77), 105–19.

McCarthy's fascination is with "the resonance of human deeds": how a single act of evil radiates and affects the entire human community. In *Orchard Keeper*, Rattner's murder is the connecting act. Ownby and Sylder are both "anomic types"—they hold "conservative" ideals of "individualistic strength and destiny." In this book, "the lives of men and animals enclose each other until the disparate orbits are seen as concentric," world within world. *Outer Dark* shows a fairy-tale form "warped by [a] Calvinist conception of sin and retribution"; "the two elements create a powerful version of primitivism." Culla and Rinthy's "punishment" is "eternal, mindless wandering, condemnation to life in a dark and pathless world"—a world without "centurion's authority or faith of Jesus." *Child of God* further tightens the focus on "depraved humanity." Lester is an "active agent of evil," like Adam, and the book portrays his descent into bestiality through a grotesque parody of pioneersmanship and normal life. For Lester, murder is the only means of human communication left. McCarthy's works show us that "the face of evil is, after all, a human face." *Outer Dark* and *Child of God* show "spare form" contrasting with the "richness" of their "parables."

Simpson, Lewis. "Southern Fiction." In *The Harvard Guide to Contemporary American Writing*, edited by Daniel Hoffman. Cambridge, Mass., 1979.

In *Child of God*, the loss of God leads to the loss of community and to radical individuation. No twentieth-century writer has created a novel that "emblemizes the tendency to resolve history in the self" with the "chilling precision" of McCarthy in *Child of God*. Lester is a lone protagonist in "grotesque pastoral," the "detritus of pioneer stock stranded by history in the mountains"—the inversion of Jeffersonian "self subsistent yeomanry" and an "individual locked in psychopathology of loneliness."

Young, Thomas Daniel. *Tennessee Writers*. Knoxville, 1981.

McCarthy's technique is what is often called southern gothic or grotesque. "Authors of this persuasion" are often accused of "deliberate distortion, of incongruous combinations of the monstrous and unsavory created and employed for the sole reason of evoking a desired effect." *The Orchard Keeper* contains "too much sin without redemption, too much horror that has no function but to furnish the reader a gratuitous emotional response." *Outer Dark* is more "under control"—convincing us of the "depravity of human nature." *Child of God* is the most forceful statement to date of McCarthy's basic concerns. There is "some order" in the "process of [Lester's] self-destruction"—at every stage he is forced to live on a more subhuman level. McCarthy's style ranges from "philosophically ponderous, slow and heavy, to the pared-down, effectively straightforward, disarmingly light." In these books, the "certainty of man's depravity no longer seems anything less than fundamental truth."

Index

Ahab, Captain, 119
Archer, Isabel, 126
Aries, Jacques, 92

Ballard, Lester, 53–68, 85
Barthelme, Donald, x
Bellow, Saul, x, 4
Blackmur, R. P., 11
Blake, William, 44, 132
Blood Meridian, ix, 3, 4, 116–35
Broyard, Anatole, ix

Child of God, ix, 6–7, 53–67
Coles, Robert, ix
Conrad, Joseph, 55, 119

Davenport, Guy, ix
Dedaelus, Stephen, 69
Divine Comedy, The, 39

Ellison, Ralph, ix

Faulkner, William, ix–x, 2, 5, 7, 34, 129
Fitzgerald, F. Scott, 78–79
Freud, Sigmund, 32

Great Gatsby, The, 78–79

Halpern, Daniel, ix
Heidegger, Martin, 32, 125
Hemingway, Ernest, 73, 128, 129
Heraclitus, 8, 108

James, Henry, 4, 11, 14, 126, 133
Joyce, James, 3, 21, 69, 72

Kafka, Franz, 39
Kant, Immanuel, 125
King Lear, 43
Knoxville, Tenn., x, 3, 22, 88, 106, 111, 113

Mailer, Norman, x
Maryville, Tenn., 4
Moll Flanders, 3

Nietszche, Friedrich, 83, 120

O'Connor, Flannery, x
Orchard Keeper, The, ix, 8, 10–32, 33, 64, 125
Outer Dark, ix, 1, 8, 33–52, 67, 107, 108, 111, 124

Pater, Walter, 7
Percy, Walker, 4
Pynchon, Thomas, ix

Sevier County, Tenn., 6, 22, 54, 56, 57, 67
Suttree, ix, 3, 8, 69–115, 124, 135

Updike, John, 2

Voltaire, 125

Warren, Robert Penn, ix
White Caps, 57–58
Whitman, Walt, 110
Woolf, Virginia, 14
Wordsworth, William, 10

Yeats, W. B., 83

www.ingramcontent.com/pod-product-compliance
Lightning Source LLC
Chambersburg PA
CBHW030116170426
43198CB00009B/640